THE DISNEY DAD'S SURVIVAL GUIDE

Becoming the **dad** your children need you to be.

OFFICIAL
DISNEY DAD

R.J. Aguilar, Jr., J.D.

DEDICATION

Author Mark Twain once said, **"The two most important days in your life are the day you're born and the day you find out why."** I don't recall the day I was born, but I remember very clearly the day I realized why. It was March 23, 2007, at 7:41 a.m. The very moment I became a father to my beautiful daughter, Presley. This book is dedicated to you. Thank you for giving me purpose. Thank you for making me your dad.

Contents

INTRODUCTION

The first thing you need to know about this book and its title is that it has nothing to do with the Disney Company or any of its subsidiaries. The term "Disney Dad", is defined in the Urban Dictionary as follows:

"A father who doesn't have physical custody of his child. So, to compensate for this, he makes the visitation times with his kids all about fun. The child's homework isn't done, there isn't a set bedtime, so the child stays up later than usual; the kid watches all kinds of inappropriate movies/TV/video games; the father is more like a 'friend' than a parent."

So not only for legal purposes, but also for ethical and clarification purposes, I want to emphasize that nothing in this book is intended to associate myself, my publishers, or the content of this book with the Walt Disney Company, its affiliates, its cast members, or shareholders.

However, I do intend this book to be a tool to break the stigma behind the term "Disney Dad". There is absolutely nothing wrong with being a fun and adventurous Dad. The key is to not ignore your obligations and duties as a mentor and a father to your children.

As a newly divorced dad, I was fortunate to have full custody of my daughter, while my ex focused on sobriety, and her other hidden demons. But for some they find themselves in a quiet house that once bustled with noise and laughter. The toys are now silent, lying around like relics of a world that had abruptly changed. It feels like walking into a movie theater during the end credits, the magic gone but the memories were still fresh. For me, I wasn't just navigating a new chapter; it felt like being handed a book in a language I couldn't read. The silence from my friends and family was deafening, the emptiness palpable, and I knew I wasn't alone in feeling this way.

Divorce throws you into a whirlwind of emotions and responsibilities you might never have anticipated. You're expected to be a rock for your children, a dependable provider, and maybe even a beacon of positive change. It's like juggling flaming torches while riding a unicycle blindfolded. It can be a lot. Can you stay balanced at dinner with your kids when your mind races about unpaid bills and future uncertainties? These are questions that keep you up at night, not because you're incapable but because you care so deeply about getting it right and not letting your kids down.

Then there's the role of active parenting—a term that's tossed around a lot but seldom dissected. Being an involved parent means more than just being present physically. It is about showing up emotionally and mentally. Attending your son's soccer games isn't just a tick on a checklist; it's a declaration, a silent promise that you'll always be there. Your presence is the cornerstone of their emotional stability, which forms the bedrock for their growth. When you show up, you're not just watching—they're seeing you, absorbing every ounce of your involvement as validation of your love and commitment.

In the chaotic aftermath of separation, the idea of co-parenting might seem like another daunting task. You and your ex-spouse, once partners, are now tasked with finding common ground for the sake of your child. Think of it like navigating a stormy sea together, even when your ship has split in two. It's a dance between compromise and cooperation, and yes, sometimes it feels like stepping on each other's toes. The key lies in prioritizing your child's needs above all else, putting differences aside to create a united front. This approach sets a foundation not just for effective co-parenting but for teaching your children about resilience, respect, and collaboration.

While this book aims to guide you through the labyrinth of single fatherhood, it also serves as a catalyst for your personal growth. Embracing this journey involves acknowledging your vulnerabilities, those raw moments where you feel lost or overwhelmed. It's here, in this very acknowledgment, that you find strength— an inner reservoir you didn't know existed. Personal development isn't a separate path but intertwined with your efforts as a father. It's about rediscovering who you are while striving to be the best role model for your children.

What can you expect from this book? Well, consider it a roadmap filled with practical tools, heartfelt stories, and actionable advice. Each chapter is designed to build on the last, guiding you step by step—not just to become a better parent but to rekindle your own sense of purpose and fulfillment. You will learn strategies to manage time, balance work and home life, and even tips on re-entering the dating scene without compromising your duties as a father. This book isn't just a manual; it's a companion on your journey, helping you navigate through the peaks and valleys of single fatherhood.

One thing that's crucial to remember: you are not alone. As you flip through these pages, imagine yourself as part of a larger community of fathers facing similar challenges. Picture us sharing stories, celebrating victories, and lending support when things get tough. This camaraderie infuses the experience with hope and determination, creating a network of mutual support. We're in this together, building a landscape where single fathers not only survive but thrive.

Together, we'll explore the emotional terrain of separation, delve into the complexities of co-parenting, and uncover the nuances of balancing new relationships with fatherhood duties. Whether it's learning to cope with stress, finding joy in everyday moments, or creating lasting connections with your children, this book covers it all. Embrace the journey back to emotional resilience and redefine what it means to be a successful, fulfilled, and happy single father.

So, take a deep breath. This book is your guide, your friend, and your source of inspiration. Turn the page and take the first step toward becoming the father, and the man, your children need you to be. Welcome to a community where we understand the silence, share the struggles, and celebrate the triumphs of single fatherhood. Let's embark on this transformative journey together, redefining fatherhood one page at a time.

ONE
Starting Over: Identifying Your Wounds

Starting over after a divorce is like trying to assemble Ikea furniture without the instructions – perplexing, emotional, and occasionally leading to tears or even anger. For dads, diving headfirst into post-divorce life brings an avalanche of feelings that can make even the most organized among us feel like we're spinning plates while riding a unicycle. The emotional fallout lands with a crash, leaving many navigating grief, confusion, and anger, all while trying to keep things together for their kids. It's like attempting to untangle Christmas lights you swore you'd put away neatly last year, only now they're wired with emotions.

In this chapter, we'll savor the rollercoaster of emotions and wrangle them into something manageable. We'll take a heart-to-heart look at why it's okay (and essential) to embrace those less-than-cheerful feelings and how acknowledging them is the first step toward healing. We'll explore coping strategies that range from stress-relieving activities to emotional outlets, ensuring you're equipped with practical advice to find your footing. Remember, processing these feelings isn't just good for you; it's crucial for setting a positive example for your kids. So, buckle up, because we're about to navigate the twists and turns of post-divorce life like seasoned thrill-seekers at a theme park.

Understanding the Emotional Impact of Divorce on Fathers

Divorce is a tough journey, particularly for fathers who often face unique emotional and practical challenges post-divorce. The impact on fathers extends beyond the legalities of the process, touching deep into their emotional well-being and daily lives. Understanding these effects is crucial to navigate this rocky terrain successfully.

Many fathers experience a whirlwind of emotions following a divorce including grief, anger, and confusion. Grieving the loss of a relationship can feel overwhelming and inescapably sorrowful. Anger might stem from feelings of betrayal or disappointment, while confusion can arise from adjusting to the new dynamics of life without a partner. Acknowledging these feelings is the first step toward healing. It's important to remember that these emotions are a natural response to significant change and must be addressed with care.

Processing these emotions is essential for mental well-being. Bottling up feelings can lead to heightened stress, anxiety, and even depression. Instead, allow yourself to feel and express what you're going through. Journaling can be an excellent way to sort through your thoughts and emotions. Talking to friends or joining support groups provides a shared space where feelings can be discussed openly without judgment. Seeking professional help, such as therapy, can also offer valuable tools and coping mechanisms tailored to your unique situation.

Moreover, learning effective coping strategies can significantly build resilience. Coping doesn't mean ignoring or suppressing your emotions but rather finding healthy ways to manage and live with them. Self-care practices, like maintaining physical health through exercise and proper nutrition, play a vital role. Engaging in activities you enjoy, whether it's hiking, reading, or playing sports, helps divert your mind and fosters a sense of normalcy.

Mindfulness techniques, such as meditation and deep breathing exercises, are superb for grounding yourself in the present moment and alleviating stress. These practices offer a mental break from the constant churn of negative thoughts and emotions, promoting a sense of calm and balance. It's about creating pockets of peace in your daily life, which cumulatively contribute to overall mental health.

Fathers should also consider how their emotional state affects their children. Children are highly perceptive and can easily pick up on their parents' distress. Therefore, it's crucial to address and manage your emotions not just for your well-being but also for the sake of your kids. Demonstrating healthy emotional management sets a positive example for them and creates a more stable home environment.

Children thrive on stability and predictability, so their father's emotional volatility can add to their own stress and anxiety. Expressing your emotions constructively, rather than bottling them up or letting them explode, teaches your children valuable lessons about emotional intelligence and resilience. Open communication with your kids is key. Let them know it's okay to feel sad or angry and encourage them to talk about their feelings as well.

It's also helpful to involve children in activities that promote bonding and mutual emotional support. Simple things like cooking together, playing games, or enjoying outdoor activities can strengthen your relationship and provide comfort during turbulent times. By making an effort to stay engaged and emotionally available, fathers can reassure their children that, despite the changes, they will always have a strong and loving presence in their lives.

Creating and maintaining a support network is another critical aspect. Don't isolate yourself; instead, lean on friends, family, and community resources. Joining a support group specifically for divorced fathers can provide camaraderie and shared understanding among those who've walked a similar path. These groups can offer insights, advice, and a sense of belonging when feeling alone weighs heavily.

Additionally, having professionals such as therapists, financial advisors, and lawyers in your support system can ease the multifaceted burdens of post-divorce life. A therapist can help navigate the emotional maze, a financial advisor can assist in managing new financial realities, and a competent lawyer ensures that all legal aspects are covered. Having this team not only supports your practical needs but also allows you to focus on rebuilding your life.

Planning for the future, even if uncertain, can give you something to look forward to. Setting achievable goals and taking small steps each day can provide direction and motivation. Whether it's advancing your career, picking up a new hobby, or focusing on personal development, these goals create a positive outlook and facilitate the healing process.

Remember, it's essential to set realistic expectations for yourself during this period. Divorce is a significant life change that takes time to adjust to. There will be ups and downs, and it's okay to have days where you feel less capable. Be patient with yourself; progress is often slow but steady.

Managing Personal Finances After Separation

As you step into your new life post-divorce, managing finances effectively becomes a crucial aspect to focus on, especially if you're a father. No doubt, navigating this new financial landscape can feel daunting at first, but equipping yourself with the right tools and knowledge can make all the difference. Let's dive into some practical steps you can take to ensure you're financially stable and well-prepared for the future.

First and foremost, establishing a clear budget that reflects your changed circumstances is essential. Your financial situation has likely shifted significantly, and it's important to adjust your budget accordingly. Start by reviewing your income sources and comparing them to your expenses. Be realistic and thorough – include everything from daily necessities to occasional splurges. This meticulous approach will give you a clear picture of where your money is going and where you can make adjustments.

When crafting your budget, don't forget to account for new, obligatory expenses such as child support and alimony. Understanding these responsibilities in depth is crucial. Child support payments are designed to cover basic necessities like food, clothing, and shelter for your children. Alimony, on the other hand, is meant to provide financial support to your ex-spouse, often to enable them to maintain a similar standard of living post-divorce. Familiarize yourself with the specifics of your obligations and ensure they are factored into your monthly planning.

In addition to managing mandatory payments, exploring community resources or programs for financial assistance can provide significant relief. Many communities offer programs aimed at helping single parents manage their finances, from subsidized childcare to food assistance programs. Investigate what's available in your area and take advantage of these resources – they're there to help you navigate this challenging time more smoothly.

Teaching your kids about money management might not seem immediately pressing, but it's a valuable investment in their future. As you gain control over your own finances, involve your children in age-appropriate conversations about money. This can be as simple as explaining the basics of saving and spending, or more complex topics like budgeting and investing as they get older. Not only does this prepare them for financial independence, but it also helps them understand the family's financial dynamics, fostering a sense of responsibility and cooperation.

Now, let's delve deeper into each of these steps to paint a clearer picture.

Creating a detailed budget starts with tracking your cash flow. Begin by listing all sources of income and then detail every expense. Remember to include fixed costs like rent or mortgage payments, utilities, and insurance, alongside variable expenses such as groceries, fuel, and entertainment. Don't shy away from using budgeting apps or spreadsheets; they can simplify the process and help you stay organized. By consistently updating your budget, you can identify patterns in your spending and find areas where you can cut back, freeing up funds for unexpected expenses or savings.

Speaking of savings, it's vital to build an emergency fund. Post-divorce life can bring unforeseen challenges, and having a financial cushion can provide peace of mind. Aim to save a portion of your income each month, even if it's a small amount. Over time, this fund will grow and can act as a safety net for emergencies, reducing stress and giving you greater financial flexibility.

Moving on to child support and alimony – it's not just about making payments but understanding the nuances involved. Each state has its guidelines, which determine the amount of child support based on various factors like income levels and custody arrangements. Alimony amounts can vary too, depending on the length of the marriage and the recipient's financial needs. Keeping thorough records of all payments is imperative. Documenting every transaction ensures transparency and can protect you in case of any disputes. Utilizing a co-parenting app can be incredibly useful here, providing a centralized place to store all financial communications and transactions.

Utilizing community resources can change the game when finances are tight. Look into local non-profits, government programs, and even faith-based organizations that offer assistance. These might include grants for utility bills, scholarships for children's extracurricular activities, or free financial counseling services. Sometimes, the most significant aid comes from asking around and networking within your community. Fellow single parents or support groups can provide invaluable advice and direct you to resources you might not have discovered on your own.

In addition to seeking external help, taking charge of personal finances through education and professional advice cannot be stressed enough. Consider meeting with a financial advisor to gain insights tailored to your situation. They can help you set realistic goals, create a long-term financial plan, and navigate investment opportunities. Moreover, numerous online resources, workshops, and courses can enhance your financial literacy, empowering you to make informed decisions.

Instilling financial literacy in your children is another pivotal task. Start simple by teaching them the value of money, the importance of saving, and how to differentiate between needs and wants. Encourage them to save a portion of their allowance or gift money in a piggy bank or savings account. As they grow, introduce concepts like budgeting, interest rates, and even the basics of investments. Real-world applications, such as letting them make a grocery list within a budget, can make these lessons engaging and practical.

Lastly, remember that financial management post-divorce isn't just about numbers; it's about building a secure and stable future for you and your children. Maintaining transparency and open communication with your co-parent regarding shared expenses is key to avoiding misunderstandings and conflicts. Adopting an approach that prioritizes the well-being of your children above all else will guide many of your financial decisions. Even if it means personal sacrifices at times, ensuring that your children have the support they need to thrive is paramount.

Establishing New Routines for Yourself and Your Children

Starting over after a divorce can be challenging for both fathers and their children. One of the most effective ways to navigate this transition is by establishing routines that bring stability and predictability back into their lives.

Incorporating structured daily schedules is key to easing the transition post-divorce. Consistency in daily activities—such as mealtimes, school drop-offs, and bedtimes—helps children feel secure. Knowing what to expect each day reduces anxiety and provides a comforting sense of normalcy. Fathers should aim to create a balanced schedule that includes work, household responsibilities, and quality time with their children. Simple routines like having breakfast together or reading a bedtime story can go a long way in reinforcing a stable environment.

Another powerful strategy is to engage children in creating their routines. Allowing them to have a say in what their new daily life looks like can enhance their sense of agency. Involving children in planning activities, setting goals, and making decisions helps them feel valued and part of the family unit. For instance, let your children decide which book to read before bed or what they would like for dinner one night of the week. This involvement can make the new routines more enjoyable and personalized, thus increasing the likelihood that they will stick to them.

While structure is important, it's equally vital to allow for flexibility in these routines. Life is inherently unpredictable, and rigid schedules can sometimes create additional stress. Being able to adapt and adjust plans, when necessary, teaches children that it's okay to be flexible and go with the flow. If a scheduled activity needs to be changed due to unforeseen circumstances, communicate openly with your children about it and involve them in deciding how to rearrange the plan. This flexibility fosters resilience and helps manage expectations realistically.

Regularly reviewing and adjusting routines as family dynamics change is also crucial. What works for your family now might not be as effective in a few months or years. As children grow and circumstances evolve, routines need to be revisited and modified accordingly. Perhaps a routine that was set during the initial months post-divorce needs tweaking as everyone becomes more accustomed to the new normal. Regular check-ins with your children about how the routines work for them can provide valuable insights. Make this review process a collaborative effort, ensuring that the routines remain relevant and beneficial for everyone involved.

Routines don't just offer stability; they also serve as an important tool for rebuilding relationships. Engaging in shared activities consistently helps strengthen the bond between fathers and their children. For example, a simple ritual like a weekly movie night can become a cherished tradition that children look forward to, providing much-needed continuity amidst the changes. These regular interactions reinforce the idea that while the family structure may have changed, the love and support within it remain constant.

Moreover, sustainable routines should be simple and manageable. They shouldn't feel like another chore but rather something enjoyable for both you and your children. Think of routines that naturally fit into your lifestyle and interests. If you love cooking, involve your kids in preparing meals. This could turn into a fun and educational session where they learn new skills while spending quality time with you. Remember, routines are more likely to last if they're enjoyable and meaningful.

It's also helpful to consider continuing some pre-divorce routines that your children are already familiar with. Carrying on with these traditions can provide a comforting link to their past and reduce feelings of loss and disorientation. For instance, if you always had Sunday pancake breakfasts, keep that going. Maintaining such familiar routines can significantly contribute to your children's emotional well-being by offering them a sense of continuity.

In creating and maintaining these routines, fathers must be mindful of their children's unique needs and preferences. Each child is different, and what works for one may not necessarily work for another. Therefore, it's important to observe and listen to your children, tailoring the routines to meet their specific needs. Some children might thrive on detailed schedules, while others might prefer more open-ended routines that allow for spontaneity.

Additionally, it's worth noting that routines aren't just beneficial for children; they also provide structure for fathers navigating their new roles post-divorce. Having a set schedule can help fathers manage their time more effectively and ensure that all aspects of life are attended to, from work responsibilities to personal self-care. A well-organized routine can prevent feelings of being overwhelmed and provide a clear framework for managing everyday tasks and long-term goals.

Finally, remember that implementing routines is a gradual process. It may take some time for everyone to adjust and find what works best. Patience and consistency are key. Celebrate small victories along the way, and don't be discouraged by setbacks. The goal is to create a nurturing and supportive environment that promotes stability and security for both you and your children.

Seeking Professional Support or Counseling

Embracing professional help and dismantling mental health stigma is crucial for fathers navigating life post-divorce. With societal pressures often painting a picture of stoic masculinity, many fathers might feel reluctant to seek necessary support. However, understanding and addressing personal emotional struggles is the first step towards healing and healthier relationships.

Fathers should begin by acknowledging their emotional turmoil. It's common to experience grief, anger, confusion, and depression after a divorce. Ignoring these feelings doesn't make them disappear; instead, it often exacerbates them. Fathers may notice signs such as irritability, constant fatigue, or withdrawal from social activities—all of which could indicate that professional help is needed. Recognizing these signs is not a sign of weakness but rather an important step in self-care and effective parenting.

Finding the right counselor or support group can significantly ease the process of seeking help. There are various types of counselors specializing in different areas, including family therapy, cognitive-behavioral therapy, and even specialized therapists for men. Support groups also provide an environment where fathers can share experiences and strategies with others facing similar challenges. Hearing stories from fellow fathers can create a sense of camaraderie and validate individual experiences, making the journey less isolating.

Open conversations about mental health play a pivotal role in breaking stereotypes associated with seeking help. When fathers openly discuss their mental health, they challenge the societal norms that dictate men must be emotionally invulnerable. Sharing personal experiences, whether with friends, family, or colleagues, fosters an environment of acceptance and normalizes the act of seeking help. This openness not only benefits the individual father but also contributes to a larger cultural shift towards embracing mental health care. But trust is an essential factor when choosing who you share with. Not everyone has your best interest in mind. So be careful.

Practicing counseling techniques at home can further enhance emotional intelligence and establish healthier relationships within the family. These techniques might include active listening, expressing emotions constructively, and fostering empathy. Fathers who regularly practice these skills are better equipped to manage interpersonal conflicts and build stronger bonds with their children. For example, setting aside time each week for a family check-in allows everyone to share their thoughts and feelings, reinforcing a culture of openness and emotional health.

Engaging in therapy provides valuable tools and strategies to navigate post-divorce challenges effectively. Therapists can guide fathers through processing their emotions, developing coping mechanisms, and re-establishing their identity. Techniques like mindfulness, cognitive restructuring, and stress management can be particularly helpful. By integrating these practices into daily routines, fathers create a stable foundation for themselves and their families.

It's essential to note that the absence of mental health support has far-reaching effects. Unaddressed mental health issues can manifest in physical health problems, substance abuse, and strained relationships. Children, too, are keen observers and often mimic their parents' coping mechanisms. By confronting and managing their mental health struggles, fathers set a positive example for their children, teaching them resilience and healthy emotional expression.

Moreover, societal attitudes towards mental health have been shifting, especially in light of recent global events. The increased stress and isolation brought about by the pandemic have highlighted the importance of mental well-being. As a result, more resources are now available to help fathers navigate their mental health journey. Websites such as Fathers Mental Health, Therapy for Black Men, and Man Therapy offer information and support tailored specifically for fathers.

Still, the key to a successful transition lies in prioritizing self-care. Fathers often carry the burden of being the primary provider, protector, and pillar of strength within the family. Yet, taking time to care for one's own mental health isn't a luxury—it's a necessity. Engaging in activities that promote relaxation and joy, such as exercise, hobbies, or simply spending time outdoors, can make a significant difference. Self-care enables fathers to recharge and approach their responsibilities with a refreshed and positive mindset.

To truly break the stigma surrounding mental health, continuous education and advocacy are essential. Fathers should be encouraged to attend workshops, read literature on mental health, and participate in community discussions. As awareness grows, so does the accessibility and acceptance of mental health services. This collective effort is instrumental in normalizing mental health care and ensuring that no father feels alone in his struggle.

Concluding Thoughts
Navigating life post-divorce is challenging, confusing, and occasionally leading to feelings of utter despair. But fear not brave souls; we've explored how fathers can better understand their emotional rollercoaster and emerged on the other side with some handy strategies. From acknowledging grief and anger to finding solace in journaling or support groups, the path to healing involves a mix of self-care, mindfulness, and staying

connected with your children, who are undoubtedly keen observers of your emotional state.

As we wrap up this chapter, remember that building new routines and seeking professional support can turn the chaos into a slightly more manageable mission. Whether it's maintaining a clear budget, engaging in shared activities with your kids, or consulting a therapist, each step forward helps rebuild stability and foster resilience. Above all, give yourself the grace to stumble and rise again, one small victory at a time. After all, life's new journey post-divorce might just surprise you with unexpected pockets of joy and growth.

TWO
The Power
of Co-Parenting

Co-parenting may seem like a constant battle with an enemy, but with the right strategies, it can be a harmonious dance that benefits everyone involved, especially your child. When two people who once shared everything from Netflix passwords to parenting duties decide to go separate ways, maintaining a collaborative and communicative environment is crucial. Imagine co-parenting as a battle plan to achieve a common goal—you need clear instructions, mutual effort, and maybe a bit of patience and strategy to make it work.

In this chapter, we dive into how you can set up regular check-ins with your ex to ensure you're both updated on your child's needs and milestones. You'll learn the magic of 'I' statements to keep conversations constructive and free from finger-pointing. We also explore the importance of clarifying boundaries to avoid turning discussions into emotional tug-of-wars. Lastly, we'll talk about positive reinforcement and how acknowledging each other's efforts can transform your co-parenting relationship into a supportive partnership. So, keep your sense of humor handy, and get ready to discover how effective communication can turn co-parenting into a synchronized swim rather than a chaotic splash.

Establishing Clear Communication with Your Co-Parent

Creating a healthy co-parenting relationship post-separation is no small feat. Yet, establishing a communicative environment that fosters collaborative parenting decisions is a crucial starting point. You might think it's like trying to herd cats, but with the right strategies, it can be more like organizing a dominant football team. Here's how you can make it happen.

First on the docket: regular check-ins. Imagine this scenario: You and your co-parent are two ships passing in the night, each navigating your child's needs without a clue what the other is doing. Scheduling consistent times to discuss updates and your child's needs ensures you're both sailing in the same direction. These regular meetings help to minimize misunderstandings and reduce the potential for emotional confrontations (fights).

The beauty of regular check-ins lies in their ability to create routine discussions. For example, a weekly video call or a bi-weekly coffee chat can become part of both parents' schedules, promoting predictability and stability. When both parties know there's a set time to bring up concerns or share victories, there's less scrambling and fewer surprises. It's like having a standing appointment with your dentist—except way less painful and infinitely more rewarding.

Now, let's talk about using 'I' statements. This technique can be your secret weapon in preventing defensive reactions and fostering open communication. Instead of saying, "You never pick up our child on time," try, "I feel stressed when our child isn't picked up at the agreed time." By focusing on your own feelings rather than pointing fingers, you keep the conversation open and less accusatory.

Using 'I' statements is especially important because it models effective communication for your children. They look up to their parents as role models, and witnessing calm, respectful exchanges teach them valuable conflict-resolution skills. For instance, if your child sees you say, "I feel upset when plans change last minute," they learn that it's okay to express emotions without assigning blame. This approach encourages empathy and mutual respect, building a strong foundation for better relationships all around.

Next up is clarifying boundaries. Setting clear limits and expectations helps keep conversations constructive. This step is not about drawing battle lines but about creating a safe space where productive dialogue can occur. Imagine a basketball game without any rules—a chaotic mess, right? Similarly, without boundaries, co-parenting discussions can deteriorate into unproductive arguments.

Consider pre-determined topics for discussions and agreed-upon times for these conversations. Maybe every Sunday evening is reserved for planning the week ahead, while financial discussions are kept to the first day of the month. Establishing these guidelines helps avoid veering off into personal grievances and respects each other's time and space. For example, deciding upfront that discussions about school activities should stay focused on logistics rather than past disagreements creates a healthier dynamic.

Finally, there's positive reinforcement. This might seem simple, but its impact is profound. Acknowledging your co-parent's efforts and strengths can build good-will and promote harmonious co-parenting. Picture this: you notice your co-parent went out of their way to make sure your child's science project was completed on time. Expressing gratitude by saying, "I appreciate you helping with the project; it made a big difference," fosters a cooperative spirit.

Positive reinforcement isn't just a tool for encouraging good behavior in kids; it works wonders with adults too. When both co-parents recognize and appreciate each other's contributions, it enhances the overall co-parenting experience. This mutual respect shows your children that collaboration and kindness are integral parts of any relationship.

Let's put it all together with an example. Suppose you've noticed that your child seems happier and less stressed recently. During a scheduled check-in, use 'I' statements to express this: "I've noticed our child is happier lately, and I think our regular discussions are really helping." Then, clarify boundaries by suggesting a focused discussion on extracurricular activities: "Can we talk specifically about adding a new activity during our next check-in?" Finally, don't forget positive reinforcement: "I really appreciate how well we've been working together on this."

By incorporating regular check-ins, 'I' statements, clarified boundaries, and positive reinforcement, you're transforming what could be a turbulent relationship into a structured, supportive partnership. This system doesn't just benefit the parents; it provides a stable, nurturing environment for your child to thrive.

Creating a Balanced Parenting Schedule

Creating a parenting plan that is both flexible and structured can be the magic wand transforming co-parenting into a smooth sail rather than a stormy sea. A successful parenting plan benefits both parents and, most crucially, prioritizes the child's stability. Let's dive into key elements to achieve this balance.

When it comes to collaborative schedule creation, there couldn't be a more potent starting point. Involve your co-parent right from the get-go. Imagine setting up a whiteboard session where you're not just plotting out soccer practices and school plays but also each parent's work commitments. This strategy reinforces teamwork and shared accountability. Both of you have contributions and seeing them laid out helps in understanding the real puzzle pieces at play. It's akin to assembling a jigsaw—both parties must see the entire picture to know where their piece fits best. Start by identifying fixed commitments, like school hours or extracurricular activities, then build around those anchors. Flexibility here isn't a sign of weakness; it's a demonstration of strength in collaboration.

Next on deck is incorporating children's preferences. This might sound like letting the inmates run the asylum but hear me out. Children are smart cookies—they know what they want. Asking for their input on preferred times with each parent can make them feel valued. Consider it as giving them a VIP pass to the "parenting concert." This approach makes them more willing to adhere to the arrangements because they had a hand in making these plans. It's a masterstroke of diplomacy; they're happier, hence less likely to resist the schedule. Spread the love equally, listen to their reasons, and tweak accordingly without turning it into a power struggle.

Utilizing tools and resources can turn co-parenting chaos into order. Modern problems require modern solutions, and luckily for us, there are apps designed specifically for co-parenting. Consider applications that offer shared calendars where both parents can update schedules in real-time. With these digital aids, everyone is on the same page—literally. These tools drastically reduce miscommunication because changes and updates are instantly visible to both parties. Plus, let's face it: pulling out your phone during a heated debate to show a mutual agreement can be quite the trump card. If apps aren't your style, even color-coded physical calendars can work wonders. The goal is to maintain transparent schedules easily accessed by both parents.

Regularly reviewing the schedule is another linch-pin in the co-parenting machine. Life is unpredictable;

hence, being rigid isn't practical. Set periodic check-ins—think of this like those car maintenance appointments. These can be weekly, monthly, or whatever frequency works best. The purpose is to assess what's working and what isn't, allowing room for adjustments. Maybe Johnny's new swim lessons conflict with Dad's late Friday meetings, or perhaps Mom's new job requires a shift in pick-up duties. Regular reviews demonstrate commitment to co-parenting and emphasize fostering a sense of partnership. Skip the novella-length meeting notes; keep it concise. Focus on actionable points and agree on any necessary changes.

Diving deeper, let's explore what each subpoint could look like in practice. When developing a collaborative schedule, use online templates to draft initial versions. Then meet with your co-parent to refine these timetables, considering vacations, holidays, and unforeseen events. Engage in an open dialogue where both can express their needs candidly. For instance, if one parent has rotating shifts, mark those clearly. Balance is key—don't let either party feel shortchanged.

Moving onto children's preferences, initiate family meetings where kids can voice their thoughts. Frame it positively, explaining how their input helps make the time spent together better. Watch their faces light up when asked, "Which days would you like to spend with each parent?" Their suggestions might surprise you in ways that simplify logistics beyond expectation. Document these choices plainly, so everyone sees them, promoting adherence.

Regarding tools and resources, research a few co-parenting apps together. Some top features include messaging capabilities, expense tracking, and shared document storage. Apps like OurFamilyWizard or Cozi can streamline the entire process. If digital doesn't cut it, a large wall calendar in each home works too. Synchronize them periodically to ensure they match. Create a hybrid system where important changes get texted or emailed instantly, backed by regular updates on your chosen platform.

During those schedule review sessions, first, discuss positive outcomes before diving into issues. Create an environment where feedback feels constructive rather than confrontational. Use this time to realign goals, addressing new challenges or changes in circumstances. Ensure the focus remains on the child's well-being rather than personal inconveniences. Take notes and recap decisions made to avoid any confusion later.

Flexibility coupled with structure is the bedrock of a stable parenting plan. It requires constant effort, frequent adjustments, and steadfast commitment to the child's happiness. By involving both parents in scheduling, honoring children's preferences, leveraging modern tools, and regularly reviewing plans, co-parenting can be transformed into a harmonious journey. Each step—no matter how small—demonstrates a shared dedication towards creating a nurturing environment for your kids, ensuring the little ones feel loved and supported from all sides.

Addressing Conflicts in a Healthy Manner

Managing disagreements with your ex in a constructive manner is pivotal, not only for maintaining a healthy co-parenting relationship but also for modeling positive conflict resolution behaviors for your children. By embracing strategies that prioritize collaboration and mutual respect, you can navigate conflicts more effectively. Here are some practical methods to consider:

Taking Breaks: When emotions run high during discussions, taking a break can be a game-changer. Imagine you're in the heat of an argument about which parent will take your child to the soccer game. The tempers are flaring, and it's becoming less about the soccer game and more about past grievances. Instead of letting the situation escalate, suggest a time-out. This break gives both parties a chance to cool down and gather their thoughts. It's like hitting the pause button on a movie; everyone returns with clearer minds and a fresh perspective on the issue at hand. During the break, engage in an activity that helps you relax— maybe a quick walk around the block or a couple of minutes with a mindfulness app. Resuming the conversation with this renewed calmness often leads to more rational discussions where solutions are easier to spot.

Focusing on Solutions, Not Problems: It's easy to fall into the trap of rehashing what went wrong. While it's human nature to point fingers and assign blame, this approach rarely produces productive outcomes. Picture this scenario: You're upset because your co-parent didn't inform you about a change in your child's school schedule. Instead of dwelling on how the miscommunication happened, pivot the focus to creating a system that ensures it won't happen again. Maybe set up a shared digital calendar or agree to send weekly updates via email. Shifting the conversation towards actionable resolutions not only resolves the current issue but also fosters a sense of teamwork and collaborative problem-solving. Plus, it sets a positive example for your children, showing them that even when things go awry, focusing on solutions rather than problems is the way forward.

Seeking Mediation: Sometimes, despite your best efforts, conflicts seem insurmountable. This is where mediation comes into play. Bringing in a neutral third party can provide much-needed perspective and help uncover underlying issues that might be fueling the conflict. A mediator isn't there to take sides but to guide both parents toward common ground. Suppose disagreements about holiday schedules keep spiraling into heated arguments. A mediator can facilitate a discussion that represents both views fairly, helping craft a plan that satisfies everyone involved. The presence of a third party can defuse tension and ensure communication remains respectful and focused on resolution. Mediation underscores the importance of resolving disputes peacefully, teaching your children valuable lessons about seeking help and maintaining harmony in relationships.

Ending Conversations on a Positive Note: While not every disagreement ends with both parties getting exactly what they want, it's crucial to end conversations respectfully. Consider making it a habit to conclude each discussion with a positive note, even if it's as simple as acknowledging the effort put into the conversation. For example, after agreeing on a new approach to handling pick-up times, say something like, "I appreciate us working through this together." These small gestures foster a more civil atmosphere and establish a foundation for future negotiations. This practice reassures your children that, regardless of your differences, you and your co-parents remain committed to a united front when it comes to their well-being.

Let's dive a bit deeper into why these strategies matter. First, taking breaks during heated moments isn't just about diffusing immediate tension. It's also about showing your children that emotional regulation is vital during conflicts. Kids often mimic the behaviors they observe. By watching you opt for a time-out to cool down, they learn that it's okay—and even beneficial—to step back and regain their composure before addressing a contentious issue.

Focusing on solutions rather than problems goes hand-in-hand with promoting a growth mindset. This approach teaches children that while mistakes and disagreements are inevitable, how we respond to them defines our relationships. Emphasizing solutions highlights the importance of learning from setbacks and continually striving for improvement. It's about building resilience and adaptability—skills that are incredibly valuable not just in co-parenting but in all aspects of life.

The use of mediation can be particularly powerful because it introduces the concept of seeking external assistance when necessary. Children who see their parents willingly engage in mediation understand that asking for help doesn't signify weakness but strength and wisdom. It illustrates that conflicts can often be resolved more effectively with a little professional guidance, reinforcing the value of teamwork and collaboration.

And finally, ending conversations on a positive note leaves a lasting impression. Respectful conclusions signal to children that it's possible to disagree without bitterness. They learn that relationships don't have to be perfect to be functional and loving. Even during tough times, showing gratitude and recognition for each other's efforts strengthens bonds and fosters an environment of mutual respect.

Ensuring Your Child's Needs Come First

Prioritizing children's well-being in every co-parenting decision made when co-parenting is essential. There is one central aim that should always lead the way: prioritizing the well-being of your children. This principle underpins every discussion, schedule adjustment, and emotional check-in. It's about creating a harmonious environment where children feel loved, supported, and valuable, despite the changing family dynamics. Here's how to do just that.

Centering Discussions on Children

Often, it can be tough to separate personal grievances from co-parenting discussions. Emotions run high, and it's easy for conversations to veer off into arguments about past mistakes or current frustrations with your ex-spouse. However, by keeping conversations focused on what benefits the kids the most, you can redirect disputes into constructive dialogues. For instance, instead of arguing over who gets to spend more time with them during holidays, emphasize what's best for the children. Perhaps they would enjoy a consistent holiday tradition that includes both parents. Remember, by fostering a team mentality, you prioritize their feelings and needs over personal conflicts.

For example, if your child loves soccer and has a big game coming up, make sure both parents are aware of the event and can attend if possible. This not only supports the child's interests but also shows them that their parents can work together when it counts. Encourage open communication where both co-parents share updates about school projects, extracurricular activities, and health matters. This united front reassures the child that despite any disagreements, their well-being takes precedence.

Consider Seasonal Changes and Events

Successfully navigating co-parenting schedules requires an awareness of seasonal changes and important events in children's lives. School calendars, special occasions, and vacations are milestones that can't be overlooked.

Planning these schedules with foresight makes life smoother for everyone involved, especially the children. It establishes predictable habits and ensures quality time spent with each parent.

For example, knowing that summer vacation means your child will have several weeks off school can help both parents plan trips and special activities in advance. Likewise, being mindful of exam periods or significant school events allows both parents to offer the support and presence needed during these critical times. Regularly revisiting and adjusting the schedule to reflect these changes demonstrates adaptability and commitment to the child's emotional and social needs.

Regular Check-Ins with Children
Children's feelings about their living arrangements and schedules may evolve as they grow. Regularly checking in with them about their experiences helps gauge their emotional health and provides insights necessary for making adjustments. Ask questions like, "How are you feeling about staying at Dad's this weekend?" or "Is there anything you'd like to change about our schedule?" Such inquiries reassure children that their voices matter in the decision-making process.

For instance, younger children might feel anxious about transitioning between homes frequently, while older children might struggle balancing time with parents and their growing social lives. By maintaining an open dialogue, you can identify any emotional distress early and address it effectively. This approach mitigates feelings of neglect or manipulation and strengthens the child's trust in both parents.

Modeling Unconditional Love

Showing empathy and care in relationships, especially amid disagreements, significantly benefits children. Modeling unconditional love teaches them that prioritizing love and respect over conflict is crucial. This can mean simple gestures like greeting each other amicably during custody exchanges or attending parent-teacher conferences together without tension.

Even when disagreements arise, maintain politeness and manage conflicts away from the children. They should never feel caught in between or pressured to take sides. A child who sees their parents handle differences maturely is likely to adopt similar behaviors. This modeling cultivates an environment rich in openness and dignity, which is essential for healthy emotional development.

One way to exhibit this is through non-verbal cues. Shared smiles, respectful nods, and calm tones during interactions convey a lot to a child observing their parents' co-parenting dynamics. Actions speak louder than words and demonstrating that love for your children remains the guiding force can profoundly impact a child's sense of security.

Another effective practice involves acknowledging and celebrating each other's contributions. If one parent excels in helping with homework, acknowledge it openly. Positive reinforcement builds goodwill and promotes a harmonious co-parenting relationship. Your child will see that mutual appreciation exists, reinforcing their belief in a loving and supportive family structure.

Final Thoughts

As we wrap up this chapter on co-parenting strategies, it's clear that successful collaboration requires dedication and open lines of communication. From regular check-ins to using 'I' statements, these tactics help create a supportive environment where everyone is on the same page. Remember, keeping discussions focused on your child's well-being rather than past grievances can shift otherwise tricky conversations into fruitful dialogues.

By clarifying boundaries and reinforcing positive behaviors, you're setting the stage for a partnership that benefits not just you and your ex-spouse but, most importantly, your child. A mutual commitment to their happiness and stability fosters a nurturing environment where they can thrive. So, next time you find yourself navigating the complexities of co-parenting, keep these strategies in mind—they're your toolkit for turning potential chaos into cohesive teamwork.

Keep in mind that what we are discussing here is a guideline. We know that each situation is different. The reasoning and circumstances behind your separation will differ from family to family. If you can manage to put your children first, it gets easier as time goes on. We promise.

THREE
Becoming an Active Father

Becoming an active father is essential for creating a strong, supportive bond with your children. It's not just about showing up; it's about being genuinely involved in their lives, celebrating their milestones, and helping them through challenges with empathy and humor. This chapter will delve into the various ways you can make meaningful contributions to your child's life, making every moment count.

First, we'll discuss the importance of participating in school events and activities, breaking down how your presence at these functions can significantly impact your child's confidence and social skills. From attending parent-teacher conferences to cheering at sports events, you'll learn practical tips on balancing work and parenting duties to ensure you're there for the big and small moments alike. Additionally, we'll explore how quality time, even in short bursts, can foster a deeper connection with your children. The chapter also covers supporting your children's interests and hobbies, encouraging them to pursue their passions with your wholehearted involvement. Finally, we'll talk about the significance of being present during critical life milestones, creating traditions, and capturing memories that will last a lifetime.

Participating in School Events and Activities

Attending school functions isn't just about showing up; it's about making a meaningful investment in your child's future. When you actively participate in school events, you're sending a strong message that you value their education. This involvement speaks volumes to your children, teachers, and even yourself.

For divorced or single fathers, your presence at school functions can make a world of difference. Imagine how your child feels seeing you in the audience during a school play or cheering them on at a sports event. It reassures them that they matter to you and that their achievements, no matter how small, are significant. Research indicates that students whose parents are engaged in their education tend to earn higher grades and have better social skills.

Direct communication with educators plays a vital role in this equation. By attending parent-teacher meetings, open houses, and other school activities, you create opportunities for dialogue. These conversations offer insights into your child's academic progress and behavior. You can share important information that teachers might not know, such as specific needs or concerns, enriching the learning experience. Furthermore, this partnership between home and school fosters a team approach, empowering parents and caregivers to be active participants in their child's education journey.

Connecting with fellow parents at these events is another benefit. Forming friendships and support systems with other parents can provide valuable emotional and practical support. Imagine swapping tips about balancing work, parenting, and life's challenges with people who understand what you're going through because they are walking similar paths. Plus, a bit of camaraderie and shared humor can make the whole parenting journey a little lighter.

Being an active participant in school functions also teaches your children the importance of community involvement and participation. They learn by watching you. When they see you volunteering at the school carnival or helping organize a fundraiser, they understand that being part of a community means contributing to it. It's a lesson that goes beyond the classroom, shaping them into responsible and engaged citizens. Demonstrating this commitment showcases the value of teamwork, giving them a model to emulate in their own lives.

Moreover, research has shown that parental involvement doesn't discriminate based on race or socioeconomic status. The positive impacts of engaging in your child's school life extend across different backgrounds and cultures. Whether you're bonding over shared school experiences or discussing ways to support each other's kids, these connections enrich everyone's lives.

Okay, let's take a moment to paint a picture here. Imagine you're at the school's annual Science Fair. You've taken time off work to be there, and you're walking around the gymnasium filled with baking soda volcanoes, solar system models, and homemade robots. You spot your child nervously standing next to their project. The moment they see you, their face lights up. Your presence alone boosts their confidence. You start asking questions about their project, genuinely interested and impressed. This interaction not only strengthens your bond but also encourages them to take pride in their work and strive for excellence.

Remember, attending school functions isn't just about big events like science fairs or sports days. It's also about the smaller, more frequent activities—parent-teacher conferences, holiday concerts, or even school board meetings. Each of these moments is an opportunity to show your child that you care about their world. Your attendance creates a positive feedback loop: the more involved you are, the more confident and motivated your child will become. They begin to understand that their efforts are recognized and celebrated, which can lead to better academic performance and overall well-being.

Now, let's talk logistics. Balancing work and parenting responsibilities is not easy, especially when you're flying solo. However, small adjustments in your schedule can make a big impact. For example, if you can't attend a daytime event, see if there's an evening option available. Schools are increasingly accommodating to diverse family schedules, offering virtual meetings and flexible event times. Communicating openly with your child's teachers about your availability can also help find mutually convenient times for important discussions.

Another tip is to set reminders for school events. Many schools have calendars or apps where you can sync events directly to your phone. This way, you'll never miss an important date. And don't underestimate the power of delegation! If you really can't make it, consider asking a trusted friend or family member to attend in your place and report back. The key is consistency and showing your child that you're making every effort to be involved.

Let's lighten things up a bit. Picture this: it's Field Day at school, and you've decided to volunteer. You're assigned to oversee the sack race, and things quickly get hilariously chaotic. Kids are tripping over each other, laughing uncontrollably, and you're right in the thick of it, encouraging them and maybe even joining in for a race or two. These are the moments that create lasting memories for your child. They'll look back and remember that their dad was not just present but an active and fun part of their school life.

Making Quality Time a Priority

Balancing work, social obligations, and personal interests can be quite daunting. However, carving out quality time for your children amidst a busy schedule is crucial. Doing so ensures that you actively participate in their lives, showing your commitment to their well-being.

Intentional planning is key. By setting aside specific times in your calendar dedicated solely to spending time with your children, you make sure that this quality time actually happens. This doesn't necessarily mean allocating large chunks of time; even short, regular interactions can foster a strong bond. Studies have shown that the quality of time spent with children has a more significant impact on their development than the quantity.

Let's consider some activities and methods that can help ensure these moments are meaningful. Introducing diverse activities such as cooking together or engaging in building projects can be excellent ways to connect. These activities offer opportunities for teamwork, conversation, and teaching valuable skills. Picture a scenario where you're both elbow-deep in flour, baking cookies from scratch. Not only does this provide a fun and messy bonding experience, but it also teaches your child about measurements, patience, and the joy of homemade treats.

Moreover, building projects can be equally engaging. Whether it's constructing a birdhouse or assembling a model car, such tasks require collaboration, problem-solving, and creativity. These projects create shared goals and tangible results that both you and your child can take pride in.

To create cherished memories, prioritize individual interactions tailored to your children's interests. If one child loves reading, set aside time to read together. If another enjoys soccer, dedicate time to kicking a ball around. Each child is unique, and by catering to their specific interests, you show them they are valued and understood. One-on-one time not only makes each child feel special but also provides opportunities to address their individual needs and concerns.

Even when time is limited, brief yet focused interactions can be incredibly impactful. Imagine a ten-minute chat over breakfast or a quick game of catch before dinner. These small moments, repeated consistently, build a foundation of trust and affection. Quality over quantity means that even short bursts of attention, when given wholeheartedly, can deepen your connection.

Encouraging daily rituals can also play an essential role. A bedtime routine where your child picks a book for you both to read can become a treasured part of their day. Rituals create predictability and security, which are vital for a child's emotional security. They look forward to these moments, knowing that regardless of the day's chaos, this special time is reserved just for them.

Additionally, turning off technology during these interactions ensures that your attention is undivided. In today's age of constant notifications and digital distractions, being fully present is a powerful way to show your children they are your priority. Turn off your phone, close the laptop, and immerse yourself in the activity at hand. This level of attention reaffirms your commitment and allows deeper connections to form.

It's important to approach these engagements with humor and lightheartedness. Laughter and playfulness can break down barriers and make interactions more enjoyable for both you and your children. Whether it's making funny faces while painting or joking around during dinner prep, incorporating humor makes the time together more memorable and enjoyable.

For instance, if your child chooses an activity that may initially seem mundane to you, like watching a favorite cartoon, dive into it with enthusiasm. Make popcorn, discuss the plot, and perhaps mimic the characters' voices. Your willingness to engage sincerely in their world speaks volumes about your love and commitment.

Furthermore, reinforcing positive behaviors during these moments can strengthen your relationship. Acknowledge when they complete chores without prompting or show kindness to siblings. Such reinforcement not only encourages good behavior but also builds their self-esteem and affirms your appreciation.

Engaging in outdoor activities can also be beneficial. A trip to the park, a nature walk, or simply playing catch in the backyard allows for exercise, fresh air, and the chance to explore the world together. It's an opportunity to ask questions, share stories, and really listen to what your child has to say. Nature offers a serene backdrop for these interactions, away from the usual indoor distractions.

When planning these activities, involve your children in the decision-making process. Ask them what they'd like to do during your time together. Giving them a voice in planning shows respect for their preferences and makes them more excited and invested in the activities.

Remember that it's okay if plans occasionally fall through. Life happens, and sometimes work or other responsibilities might interfere. When this occurs, communicate openly with your child. Explain the situation and reschedule the missed time. This transparency helps them understand and prepares them for real-life scenarios where flexibility is necessary.

To keep the bonding process creative and fresh, mix up the activities regularly. One weekend could be a baking session, the next could be a movie marathon, followed by a DIY craft project. Variety keeps the experiences exciting and gives you both something to look forward to.

Finally, don't underestimate the value of simple, everyday interactions. Sitting together during meals, sharing stories about your day, or even grocery shopping together can be moments of connection. These routines, though seemingly ordinary, are the threads that weave your relationship tighter.

Supporting Your Children's Interests and Hobbies

Fatherhood is an adventure, and what better way to explore this journey than to dig deep into your children's individual passions and interests? Encouraging fathers to actively engage with their children's hobbies can lead to tremendous growth for both parties. It's about showing up, diving in, and fostering a connection that's rooted in shared experiences.

First and foremost, attending their games, performances, or competitions is a game changer when it comes to building their self-esteem. Imagine the shining eyes of your child searching the crowd for you during their soccer match or school play. Your presence alone can reinforce that they matter, and you're there to witness their moments of triumph (and even their stumbles). Think of it as becoming their biggest fan, someone who cheers them on both figuratively and literally. Plus, chanting embarrassing yet supportive slogans is practically a dad rite of passage.

But don't stop at just being a spectator. Sharing in their hobbies, even those that feel as foreign as learning an alien dialect, is crucial. If your kid is passionate about painting miniatures or has taken an intense interest in birdwatching, throw yourself into it with gusto. Whether or not you have a clue what you're doing, your effort to understand and participate validates their passions. It's like saying, "Hey, I see you, and I think what you're into is awesome." In return, you'll find yourself bonding over shared victories and hilarious failures—both of which make for excellent stories around the dinner table.

Encouraging your children to take healthy risks is another vital aspect of nurturing their interests. When they approach you with a wild idea, like trying out for the school's debate team despite never having spoken in public, support them. Healthy risks are great confidence boosters. They teach resilience, push boundaries, and help kids discover new strengths. Your role here is like being a safety net; you're there to catch them if they falter but also to remind them that falling is part of the process. Allowing them the space to challenge themselves shows trust in their abilities and fosters independence.

Then there's facilitating access to training or materials for their interests. If your daughter dreams of becoming a pianist, help her get there by finding a teacher, getting a keyboard, or simply setting aside time for practice. You don't need a hefty wallet; sometimes it's about looking for community resources or swapping skills within your social circle. Maybe your neighbor can offer guitar lessons in exchange for you teaching their kid how to swim. The goal is to show your commitment to their growth. Kids value tangible efforts; it's one thing to say you support them, but quite another to rearrange your schedule for a recital or artistically butcher a family room wall just to hang up their artwork.

Believe it or not, the act of engaging in your child's interests can enrich your life too. These activities open doors to new experiences and perspectives that you might not encounter otherwise. Ever found yourself at a cosplay convention giving your best superhero pose or struggling to keep up in a dance-off? Embracing these moments not only builds memories but also showcases flexibility and willingness to grow—traits that rub off on your kids.

Creating an environment where your children feel supported empowers them to pursue what they love with confidence. This active involvement sends a strong message that their interests are worthwhile. Support doesn't have to be perfect; it's the genuine effort that counts. Life gets busy, schedules clash, and energy may run low, but prioritizing these engagements creates lasting impressions. Remember, it's not about grand gestures; small actions often speak louder. Show up at their events, engage in their quirks, encourage their explorations, and provide necessary tools. Fathers who invest in their children's passions cultivate relationships rooted in mutual respect, joy, and endless possibilities. So go ahead, dive into their world, and watch both of you transform.

Being Present During Significant Milestones

Being an active father is about more than just showing up; it requires genuinely engaging and supporting your children through their critical life events to create lasting memories and foster emotional development. Witnessing significant milestones, establishing traditions around key events, providing support during difficult times, and capturing shared experiences are essential components of this process.

Witnessing significant milestones like graduations, birthdays, or achievements in hobbies and sports can profoundly reinforce emotional connections with your children. Imagine the pride on your child's face as you cheer them on at their first soccer goal or beam with joy at their graduation ceremony. These moments, no matter how big or small, are pivotal for bonding. They deliver a strong message that you value and celebrate their accomplishments, which boosts their self-esteem and emotional security.

As fathers, it's crucial to establish traditions around key events to add meaning and deepen family ties. For instance, if your child wins an award, make it a tradition to have a special dinner to celebrate each achievement. Or perhaps every holiday season, you could embark on a mini-road trip to visit relatives. These recurring activities provide stability and something to look forward to, creating a thread of memorable experiences that solidify the family bond over time.

Supporting your children during difficult times showcases unconditional support and strengthens trust between you and your kids. Let's say your child is dealing with bullying at school. It's essential to be there not just physically but emotionally, listening to their concerns, offering comfort, and working together to find solutions. The same goes for helping them through academic struggles or the heartbreak of a lost friendship. Your presence and reassurance during these times build a foundation of trust and demonstrate that they can rely on you, no matter what.

Capturing memories through photos, notes, or discussions helps preserve these shared experiences and reinforces your involvement in their lives. For example, maintaining a photo album of family vacations or special occasions can serve as a cherished keepsake that your child will look back on fondly. Writing letters or keeping a journal of your thoughts and feelings during significant events can offer your child a window into your perspective and strengthen the emotional connection. Discussing past shared experiences during casual conversations also keeps these memories alive, fostering a sense of continuity and history within the family.

Fathers, particularly those navigating co-parenting post-divorce or balancing new relationships, must prioritize attending major life events. Sharing these moments speaks volumes about your commitment and love. Even when challenges arise, such as conflicting schedules or geographical distance, it's essential to find ways to be present. Perhaps you can't attend every event in person, but a heartfelt video call or a thoughtful message can still convey your unwavering support and concern.

Celebrating achievements should be deliberate and thoughtful. Make sure to acknowledge your child's hard work and effort, not just the end result. This approach not only encourages a growth mindset but also emphasizes the value of perseverance and dedication. Consider adopting a ritual where, after any milestone, you go out for ice cream or watch their favorite movie together. These simple yet meaningful acts can turn achievements into treasured traditions.

Creating new traditions doesn't require grand gestures but rather consistent and genuine efforts. Start by identifying activities that resonate with both you and your child. It could be as straightforward as having a Saturday morning breakfast ritual, where you cook pancakes together while catching up on the week's events. Over time, these routines become cornerstones of your relationship, providing a sense of predictability and comfort for both of you.

When your child faces adversity, being there is crucial. Children often struggle with issues that may seem trivial to adults but are monumental in their world. Whether it's dealing with a failing grade, a falling out with friends, or anxiety about an upcoming exam, your support can make all the difference. Approach these situations with empathy and patience. Listen actively without immediately jumping to solutions—sometimes, they need a sounding board rather than a fix-it hero. Let them know that it's okay to feel vulnerable and that you're there to help navigate their emotions and challenges.

Taking steps to support your child through tough times can also mean advocating for them when necessary. Suppose your child is experiencing difficulties at school that require intervention. In that case, collaborating with teachers or seeking professional help shows your commitment and willingness to go the extra mile for their well-being.

While capturing memories, aim to involve your child in the process. Invite them to help with organizing family photos or creating scrapbooks. This activity becomes another avenue for bonding and allows them to reflect on shared experiences positively. Moreover, discussing these memories can open up opportunities for deeper conversations about their feelings and perspectives, further enriching your relationship.

Balancing responsibilities as a father with other aspects of life, such as work and personal relationships, can be challenging. However, making time for your child during crucial moments demonstrates that they are a priority. It might mean rearranging your schedule or making sacrifices, but the long-term benefits to your relationship with your child are worth it.

Closing Remarks

Engaging in your child's life isn't just about marking dates on a calendar. It's about being there, cheering them on at school events, and sharing the daily highs and lows. Whether it's watching a Science Fair project come to life or participating in a chaotic sack race, these moments create lasting memories and teach your child the value of community and participation. Your involvement sends a clear message: you prioritize their world, boosting their confidence and motivation.

Fostering quality time with your child might seem challenging amidst busy schedules, but it's more about consistency and intention than grandeur. Cooking together, building projects, or simply chatting over breakfast can build strong bonds. Tailoring activities to their interests shows you genuinely care. Even small interactions, like turning off tech for undivided attention or injecting humor into daily routines, make a big difference. These efforts reinforce that your child is a priority, strengthening your relationship and contributing to their overall well-being.

FOUR
Dating as a Single Dad

Dating as a single dad is an obstacle that is necessary if you want an opportunity to move on with your own life—it's challenging but certainly not impossible. You've got to balance your parenting duties with the desire to build a new romantic relationship, all without dropping any of the responsibilities that come with either role. Your kids are always watching, learning how to handle life's various demands by observing you. In this chapter, we'll delve into strategies to make sure neither your dating life nor your parenting duties fall by the wayside.

Navigating the complex tapestry of single parenthood and dating requires a thoughtful approach, and that's precisely what we're going to explore here. From knowing when and how to introduce your new partner to your children, to arranging low-pressure joint activities that foster a comfortable environment for everyone, we'll cover it all. We'll discuss how to communicate openly with your kids about your new relationship, ensuring their emotional security isn't compromised. Additionally, we'll look at time management techniques that will help you give both your children and your romantic interest the attention they deserve. By the end of this chapter, you'll have a toolbox full of tips and tricks to seamlessly integrate dating into your parenting life.

Introducing a New Partner to Your Children Safely

Introducing a new partner to your children is an essential step that requires careful consideration and planning. Balancing dating with parenting comes with its challenges and ensuring that both your new partner and your children are prepared for the potential of a blended family dynamic is crucial. With that in mind, make sure the person you are introducing to your life is going to be a serious and long term relationship. Here's how you can navigate this delicate process.

Introduce a New Partner Only When a Relationship is Serious

One of the most important steps in blending families is timing. Introducing your children to a parade of short-term partners can lead to emotional confusion and instability. Instead, only consider making introductions when you're confident that the relationship has long-term potential. This approach minimizes the risk of your children forming attachments to someone who might not be around for the long haul. Children thrive on stability, so let them see only those people who are likely to become part of their lives permanently, not a "hook up" or "friend with benefits".

Clearly Communicate the New Relationship to Your Children

Once you've decided that your relationship is serious enough to introduce your partner to your children, it's crucial to communicate with them openly and honestly. Use age-appropriate language to explain the situation. Younger children may need simpler explanations, while older ones will appreciate a more detailed conversation. Explain who your new partner is and why they are important to you. This transparency helps build trust and ensures that your children understand what's happening without feeling blindsided.

For example, if you have younger kids, you might say, "Daddy has a new friend, and I'd like you to meet her because she's very special to me." For older children, you could expand on this by saying, "I've been seeing someone for a while, and I think it's time you met her. We care about each other a lot, and I believe you'll like her too." Be aware of the circumstances. For example, if the person you're dating now happens to be part of the cause of your separation, being sensitive to that fact is important.

Arrange Low-Pressure Joint Activities
The first meeting between your new partner and your children should be in a relaxed environment. Avoid formal or high-pressure settings which might make everyone anxious. opt for casual, fun activities that allow natural interactions. A day at the park, a pizza night at home, or a simple trip to the ice cream shop can work wonders. These low-pressure settings provide an opportunity for everyone to get to know each other without the stress of forced conversations.

During these activities, you can observe how your children and your partner interact and ensure that the environment remains comfortable for all. Additionally, engaging in shared activities helps break the ice and fosters initial bonding moments in a less intimidating way. Choosing a new partner that will fit well into your little family is essential. If there is conflict, pay close attention to the dynamics. And remember your children are your priority at this point.

Be Attentive to Your Children's Feelings
Children react differently to significant changes, and it's essential to be observant and sensitive to their emotions throughout the introduction process. Pay close attention to their verbal and non-verbal cues. Are they excited? Anxious? Reluctant? Address any concerns proactively to validate their feelings. Let them know that it's okay to feel a mix of emotions and that their feelings matter to you. The same observations need to be attributed to the actions and emotions of your new partner as well.

Open up a dialogue where they can share their thoughts and ask questions. Assure them that they remain your top priority and that adding a new person to your life doesn't mean they are being replaced. Regularly check in with them after meetings to gauge how they are feeling and to provide reassurance.

Consider Timing
When introducing a new partner, timing is everything. Ensure that both you and your children have had adequate time to adjust to the separation or loss of a

previous partner. Rushing into new introductions can cause additional stress and emotional strain. Wait until you've established a stable routine, and your children have shown signs of adjusting well to your current family structure.

By giving everyone time to heal and adapt, you create a stronger foundation for the new relationships to develop. It's better to delay introductions than to cause undue emotional turmoil by moving too quickly.

Setting Expectations

It's also essential to set realistic expectations for how the new family dynamics will unfold. Have conversations with your children about what they can expect from your new partner and vice versa. Clarify that your new partner isn't there to replace the other parent but to add to their support system.

Similarly, discuss your expectations with your new partner. Make sure they understand the importance of building a bond with your children slowly and respectfully. They should be prepared to face some resistance initially and handle it with patience and understanding. Clear communication of roles and expectations can ease the transition for all parties involved. Don't be afraid to face any conflicts that may arise. It's understandable that not all new partners will be a good fit. Be prepared to make changes if it's for the benefit of your relationship with your kids.

Planning Joint Activities

To foster a good relationship between your new partner and your children, plan regular joint activities that encourage bonding. Activities that involve teamwork and collaboration, such as playing board games, sports, or even cooking a meal together, can help strengthen these new relationships. The goal is to create positive experiences that your children can associate with your new partner, building trust and affection over time.

Avoid overwhelming your children with too many joint activities too soon. Gradually increase the frequency and complexity of these activities as comfort levels rise. This gradual approach ensures that the transition feels natural rather than forced.

Monitoring Reactions

Finally, continuously monitor how your children are reacting to the new addition to your family. Be vigilant about any changes in their behavior, mood, or academic performance. If you notice negative reactions, take them seriously and address them promptly. Seek professional guidance if necessary to help navigate particularly challenging transitions.

Remember, blending a family is a journey that takes time, patience, and effort. By paying close attention to your children's needs and emotions, you can foster a supportive environment where all members of the new family dynamic can thrive.

Balancing Time Between Dating and Parenting

Managing time effectively as a single dad is another challenge you should take seriously. Blending families or introducing somebody new is not a game. It's a life altering event in the life of your child. You need to balance your commitments to dating and parenting, ensuring both aspects thrive without one overshadowing the other.

First and foremost, prioritize quality time with both your children and your romantic interest. The key is to make sure you set aside specific times for each. Consider alternating between family activities and date nights. For instance, one weekend you might take your kids out for a fun day at the park or an ice cream outing, followed by a quiet dinner or movie night the next weekend with your partner. This way, both your children and your partner get the attention they deserve. It's all about making these moments count rather than focusing on the quantity. As you nail down this rhythm, you'll find it much easier to give everyone the best of you. If there is shared custody, take advantage of your child free time to nurture the new relationship away from the eyes and ears of your kids.

Next, implementing a family calendar can be a game-changer. This isn't just any calendar—it's a master schedule that includes everything from school runs to soccer practice, playdates, and yes, dating-related activities. Using Google Calendar or even a good old-fashioned wall planner can bring structure to chaos. It lets you visually map out where your time goes, helping you spot potential conflicts before they arise. Plus, it allows for flexibility; if an unexpected parent-teacher meeting pops up, you can easily shuffle things around without losing your grip on either front.

One critical aspect of this balancing act is discussing your dating commitments with your partner. Transparency is your friend here. Sit down together and talk about what your typical week looks like, highlighting when you're available and when you're fully booked with dad duties. Mutual respect for each other's schedules will go a long way in avoiding conflicts. Both parties need to understand that your responsibilities as a father are a top priority, and getting on the same page early on helps set realistic expectations.

To further ease the stress of planning dates, lean on trusted family members or friends for childcare. Having a reliable support network can provide peace of mind, knowing your kids are well taken care of while you're out. Whether it's asking a grandparent to babysit or arranging a playdate with a close friend's child, this support system acts as a buffer, allowing you to focus on enjoying your time out without constantly checking your phone. Remember, building a village is essential for lightening the parenting load.

Setting Boundaries with New Relationships
Navigating the dating world as a single dad can be stressful and sometimes includes feelings of guilt and failure. It's no small feat, but establishing healthy boundaries early on can safeguard your parenting responsibilities

and foster a strong romantic connection. Boundaries are essential in ensuring that both aspects of your life—a new relationship and your role as a father—are nurtured without one overshadowing the other. Here's how to set those all-important boundaries to protect both your children and your budding romance.

First, let's talk about sharing your intentions in the new relationship. When diving into the dating pool, transparency is your best friend. From the start, let your new partner know about your role as a father. Be open about your daily routines, parenting duties, and the times when these responsibilities take precedence. This level of honesty sets the stage for realistic expectations and builds trust. For instance, saying something like, "My kids are my priority, and I want you to understand and respect that from the beginning," can go a long way in avoiding misunderstandings down the line.

Now, let's address the non-negotiable nature of your parenting time. As much as you may want to spend every free moment with your new partner, your kids require your unwavering attention during certain periods. Make it crystal clear when your parenting time is off-limits. For example, if Wednesday evenings are reserved for homework help or weekend mornings are for soccer practice, communicate these commitments firmly. By setting explicit expectations, you prevent conflicts and ensure that your children don't feel neglected. This approach also showcases your reliability and dedication as a parent—qualities that are attractive to a potential partner. At least they should be to the right partner.

Furthermore, ensure your new partner understands their supportive role without stepping into parental territory. It's crucial that your romantic interest knows they're not expected (or allowed) to adopt a disciplinary role or make decisions for your child. Instead, their position should be one of emotional support, complementing your parenting rather than complicating it. For example, if you have a routine for bedtime stories, it's your job to maintain that ritual. Your partner can provide support by offering encouragement to your child or lending a listening ear if you need to vent about parenting challenges. Establishing this clear division prevents any blurring of lines that could confuse your child or cause friction in your relationship.

Boundaries aren't static; they need to evolve as relationships grow and children adapt. Periodically reviewing and reassessing these boundaries is essential. As your romantic relationship progresses and your child's needs change, sit down with your partner to discuss any necessary adjustments. Maybe initially, Sunday dinners were sacred family time, but over time, your child becomes comfortable enough to occasionally share this space with your new partner. Positive negotiations like these demonstrate flexibility and a willingness to adapt, which fosters a healthy, balanced environment for everyone involved. Aim for regular check-ins to ensure all parties are content and their needs are being met.

Balancing dating while being a dedicated single dad requires a fine-tuned approach to boundary-setting. Each of these steps plays a vital role in maintaining harmony between your parental duties and your romantic endeavors. Remember, the goal isn't to create rigid walls but to build a framework that supports both areas of your life, allowing them to flourish in tandem.

One key aspect of this balancing act is recognizing when to involve your partner in your child's life. While the ultimate goal may be to blend your new relationship seamlessly with your family dynamics, rushing this process can backfire. Introduce your partner slowly and thoughtfully. Start with casual interactions and gradually increase their involvement as your child becomes more comfortable. This method ensures a smoother transition and minimizes potential feelings of intrusion or jealousy from your child or even from your new partner.

It's equally important to keep the lines of communication open with your kids. They deserve to know what's happening in their family life and why certain boundaries are in place. Explain to them that while they are your top priority, you also have personal needs and relationships to nurture. Use age-appropriate language to convey this message, ensuring they feel valued and understood. For example, tell your younger kids, "I love spending time with you, and I also enjoy getting to know new people. But our special time together remains just as important." This clarity helps them comprehend and respect the boundaries you've established.

Another critical guideline is maintaining consistency in your boundaries. Kids thrive on routine, and having a predictable pattern can significantly reduce stress and anxiety. Stick to your established schedules and rules, regardless of external pressures. If Friday night is movie night with your kids, don't cancel it last minute for a date. By honoring these commitments, you reinforce their importance and demonstrate your reliability. Consistency not only benefits your children but also showcases to your partner your steadfast dedication to your parental role.

Role modeling is another powerful tool in teaching and reinforcing boundaries. Children learn by observing, so embody the behaviors and attitudes you wish to instill. If you expect your child to respect your dating boundaries, show them that you respect their boundaries too. For instance, if your child has a "no interruptions during study time" rule, adhere to it diligently. Equally, display respect towards your partner's boundaries in front of your children. This mutual respect fosters an environment where boundaries are seen as beneficial and necessary for healthy relationships.

Finally, embrace the journey of setting and maintaining boundaries with humor and patience. Parenting is already a challenging endeavor, and adding dating to the mix can sometimes feel overwhelming. Approach this new chapter with a sense of adventure and a willingness to learn from missteps. Celebrate the small victories, whether it's successfully coordinating a date night around your child's schedule or finding the perfect balance between family time and romantic engagements. A positive attitude and a dose of humor can make the entire process more enjoyable for everyone involved.

Communicating Your Status as a Single Parent

Dating as a single dad can be a unique and challenging experience, but honesty from the start is essential to fostering authentic connections with potential partners. Being open about your status as a single father early in the relationship helps establish trust and sets realistic expectations for both parties. This openness not only builds a strong foundation of trust but also removes any unwelcome surprises that might later disrupt the developing relationship.

One of the first things you should communicate to potential partners is that you are a single father. It's important to share this information early on because it allows your partner to understand and appreciate your responsibilities and commitments. It's helpful to weave this into casual conversation rather than making it an overly formal announcement. For example, if you're sharing stories about your daily life, mention activities you do with your children. Transparency about your parenting status can set the stage for trust and ensure that both you and your potential partner are on the same page from the beginning.

Emphasizing the joys and rewards of being a father during dating conversations can also foster mutual appreciation. Sharing anecdotes about meaningful moments with your kids or discussing what you love about being a parent shows your dedication and highlights the positive aspects of your life. This not only makes your role as a father more relatable but also invites your date to see the parts of your life that bring you happiness and fulfillment. Celebrating these joys together can create a bond and help your partner appreciate the integral role your children play in your life.

Additionally, being upfront about your commitments and daily routine as a father is crucial to setting clear expectations for availability. When you explain your schedule, including when you have childcare responsibilities, your potential partner gains insight into your life and understands when you can and cannot be available. For instance, clarify times when you need to pick up your children, assist with homework, or spend quality family time. By doing so, you prevent misunderstandings and help your partner see how they might fit into your life.

For example, consider explaining that your availability for spontaneous outings might be limited due to your parenting responsibilities. Clarifying that while you value spending time with your partner, you must prioritize your children's needs to ensure that your partner respects your commitments without feeling neglected. This kind of transparency creates a balanced relationship where expectations are aligned, reducing the likelihood of frustration or disappointment.

Moreover, inviting potential partners to ask questions regarding your parenting and family life can create deeper understanding and trust. Encouraging questions demonstrates that you are open and willing to share, which fosters a supportive environment for your relationship. It allows your partner to gain a clearer picture of what your day-to-day life looks like and how they might integrate into it. Offering insights into your children's personalities, hobbies, and routines can humanize them and make your partner feel more connected to your family dynamics.

For instance, you could say, "Feel free to ask me anything about my kids or our routine. I want you to feel comfortable and know as much as you'd like." This invitation not only opens the door to meaningful conversations but also shows that you are considerate of your partner's curiosity and comfort level.

It's worth noting that being raised by a single parent who dates can significantly impact children. Continuously introducing new relationships too soon can have negative emotional and psychological effects on children, including trust issues and attachment problems. Therefore, it's important to balance your dating life with sensitivity towards your children's emotional well-being. Ensuring that your kids feel secure and included in your decisions can mitigate potential issues and create a healthier environment for everyone involved.

Discussing your schedule openly with your partner also guides them on when they can expect to spend time with you without feeling sidelined by your parental duties. Being specific about your routine and highlighting windows of time dedicated to dating can help your partner plan accordingly. For example, you might explain that your weekends are usually reserved for family activities, but you are available for dates during weekday evenings after your children are asleep. Clear communication about your schedule prevents misunderstandings and ensures that your partner knows when they can look forward to spending quality time with you.

By integrating these strategies, you create a balanced approach to dating that respects both your role as a father and your desire for a fulfilling romantic relationship. Authenticity and clear communication serve as the cornerstones for building trust, appreciation, and mutual respect between you and your potential partner. Moreover, involving your partner in discussions about your parental responsibilities fosters a collaborative atmosphere where both parties can feel valued and understood.

Concluding Thoughts

In this chapter, we've tackled the challenging yet rewarding task of balancing dating with parenting responsibilities. We explored practical strategies like setting realistic expectations, maintaining clear communication, and introducing new partners thoughtfully to ensure that both your romantic relationship and your bond with your children flourish harmoniously. By prioritizing stability and creating a supportive environment, you can navigate these dual roles without compromising on either front.

As you embark on this balancing act, remember that patience and flexibility are key. It's essential to honor your commitments as a father while also making time for personal happiness and growth. By gradually integrating your new partner into your family life and keeping open lines of communication with your kids, you set the stage for a positive and healthy family dynamic. Ultimately, it's about finding that sweet spot where everyone feels valued and supported, leading to a richer, more fulfilling experience for all involved.

FIVE
Building Emotional Resilience in Yourself

Building emotional resilience is like assembling a toolbox for life's inevitable storms. Whether it's dealing with the ups and downs of co-parenting or managing the daily grind as a single dad, having the right tools can make all the difference. Emotional resilience isn't something you're born with; it's developed through practices that strengthen your mental and emotional muscles. This chapter dives into some practical techniques you can use to build this resilience, making you more adaptable and ready to face challenges head-on.

In this chapter, you'll explore the world of mindfulness and self-care, two essential elements in building emotional resilience. From the simplicity of deep breathing exercises to the subtle art of body scans, you'll learn how to bring your mind back to the present and reduce anxiety. We'll also delve into creating a personalized self-care routine that goes beyond bubble baths and indulges in activities that genuinely nurture your soul. Additionally, there are sections on how to limit negativity by reframing thoughts and setting boundaries to protect your emotional energy. Get ready to discover strategies that not only enhance your well-being but also make you a stronger, more resilient father.

Practicing Mindfulness and Self-Care

Building emotional resilience is a crucial aspect of thriving as a divorced father. One of the most effective ways to build this resilience is by incorporating mindfulness and self-care into your daily routine. These practices can help manage stress, improve your overall well-being, and make you more capable of handling the ups and downs of co-parenting and single life.

First, let's dive into understanding mindfulness. Mindfulness is all about being present in the moment without judgment. It's easier said than done, but with practice, it can become second nature. Techniques like deep breathing and body scans are excellent starting points. Deep breathing may seem trivial, but it's a powerful tool. When you're feeling overwhelmed or anxious, taking slow, deep breaths can calm your nervous system almost instantly. Try this: sit in a comfortable position, close your eyes, and take a deep breath in through your nose, hold it for a few seconds, then slowly exhale through your mouth. Repeat this process several times, focusing solely on your breath. This simple exercise can bring your mind back to the present, easing anxiety and helping you focus better.

Body scans are another useful technique. This involves mentally scanning your body from head to toe, paying attention to any areas of tension or discomfort. Lie down in a quiet place and close your eyes. Start at your head and work your way down, acknowledging each part of your body. Are your shoulders tense? Is your back aching? By identifying these areas, you can consciously relax them, reducing physical and mental stress. Practicing body scans regularly can increase your awareness of how stress affects your body, making it easier to address and manage these issues before they escalate.

Creating a self-care routine is equally important. Self-care isn't just about bubble baths and face masks— though those can be nice too. It's about prioritizing activities that nourish your mind and body. Simple activities like reading, journaling, or taking long walks can make a significant difference. For instance, setting aside 20 minutes a day to read a book (like this one) can be incredibly fulfilling. It not only provides an escape from daily stressors but also stimulates your mind.

Journaling is another fantastic self-care activity. It allows you to express your thoughts and feelings freely, providing a safe space to vent and process emotions. Start by writing about your day, your experiences, and how you feel. Over time, you might notice patterns in your thinking or recurring sources of stress. Recognizing these patterns can help you address underlying issues and find healthier ways to cope.

Long walks are a great way to combine physical activity with mindfulness. Walking in nature not only benefits your physical health but also provides an opportunity to clear your mind. Leave your phone behind, listen to the sounds around you, and let your thoughts run free. This can be particularly refreshing if you've been cooped up indoors or dealing with stressful situations.

Limiting negativity is another critical aspect of building emotional resilience. Negative thoughts and influences can drain your energy and make it challenging to stay positive. One effective strategy is to reframe negative thoughts into constructive ones. For example, instead of thinking, "I'm a terrible parent," try reframing it to, "I'm doing my best, and I can always improve." This shift in perspective can change how you perceive challenges and setbacks, making them seem more manageable.

Reducing negative influences also means being mindful of the company you keep and the media you consume. Surround yourself with supportive friends and family who uplift you, rather than those who bring you down. If certain social media accounts or news outlets trigger negative emotions, consider unfollowing or limiting your exposure to them. It's essential to create a positive environment that fosters growth and resilience.

Setting boundaries is another vital component of self-care and emotional resilience. As a divorced father, you might feel pulled in multiple directions—between work, co-parenting, and your personal life. Learning to say no is crucial. It helps protect your emotional energy and ensures you have enough left for what truly matters. For instance, if you're constantly agreeing to extra work hours that leave you exhausted, it's time to set boundaries. Politely decline additional tasks that aren't essential and explain that you need time to recharge and spend with your children.

Setting boundaries also applies to social interactions. You might feel obligated to attend every social event or meet every friend who asks, but it's okay to prioritize your needs. If you're feeling drained, it's perfectly acceptable to decline an invitation and take some time for yourself instead. Remember, taking care of your emotional well-being enables you to be a better father and role model for your children.

Incorporating these practices into your daily routine can significantly enhance your ability to cope with stress and emotional upheaval. Mindfulness techniques like deep breathing and body scans can provide immediate relief from anxiety and improve focus. Creating a self-care routine with activities such as reading, journaling, or taking long walks can nourish your mind and body. Limiting negativity by reframing negative thoughts and reducing harmful influences can foster a more positive outlook on life. Finally, setting boundaries protects your emotional energy and ensures you have time for what truly matters.

Overcoming Feelings of Loneliness and Isolation

Combatting loneliness and isolation following a divorce is an essential step for any father aiming to build emotional resilience. The first step in this journey involves recognizing the natural feelings of loneliness that often come with the end of a significant relationship. It's common to feel isolated after a divorce, and acknowledging these emotions is crucial for mental health. Avoiding or denying these feelings can lead to deeper issues like depression or anxiety. Accepting these emotions without judgment is a vital part of the healing process. You should also be aware of the effects this can have on your health, blood pressure, and reactive behavior.

While it may be uncomfortable to face these feelings head-on, understanding their impact on your mental health can provide motivation. Loneliness doesn't just affect the mind; it can also have physical consequences. Stress-related ailments, such as headaches, digestive issues, and lowered immunity, are often linked to prolonged feelings of isolation. Recognizing that these sensations are both normal and serious can empower you to seek remedies actively.

One effective strategy to combat loneliness is reaching out to friends and family. Re-establishing connections with those who care about you is not only comforting but also provides a support system. You might feel hesitant to reach out, fearing judgment or pity, but remember that genuine relationships are based on mutual care and support. Initiating contact doesn't have to be a grand gesture; simple acts like sending a text or arranging a coffee meet-up can go a long way. Regular interactions help rebuild a sense of belonging and can significantly alleviate feelings of isolation.

Support groups specifically geared towards divorced parents or single fathers can be particularly beneficial. These communities offer a space where members share similar experiences and challenges, making it easier to relate and feel understood. Parenting communities, whether online or local, can also provide invaluable advice and camaraderie. Being around others who've faced similar struggles reinforces that you're not alone in this journey, fostering a sense of solidarity and support.

Finding new social circles is another key aspect of overcoming isolation. Engaging with other fathers through local or interest-based groups can open doors to meaningful friendships. Consider joining hobby clubs, sports teams, or even classes that interest you. Whether it's a local basketball league or a book club, shared interests create natural bonding opportunities. Participating in activities that you enjoy not only helps in meeting new people but also brings joy and fulfillment into your life, which is crucial during challenging times.

Volunteering can be a highly rewarding way to mitigate feelings of isolation. Community service allows you to give back, which can be intrinsically fulfilling. It creates opportunities to interact with diverse groups of people, helping you forge new connections while contributing positively to society. Whether it's mentoring youngsters, helping out at a food bank, or participating in community clean-ups, giving your time and effort fosters a sense of purpose and belonging. Plus, volunteering often attracts kind-hearted individuals, increasing the likelihood of building compassionate and supportive friendships.

Above all, combating loneliness post-divorce revolves around action and engagement rather than passivity. Feelings of isolation thrive when left unchecked in silence. By actively seeking out supportive environments and engaging in fulfilling activities, you can create a network of connections that buffer against loneliness. Overcoming the inertia to reach out, participate, and volunteer can be challenging, but each small step brings you closer to a more connected and fulfilling life.

Engaging in Physical Exercise for Mental Health

Picture this: It's been a long, grueling day at work. Deadlines are looming, and stress levels are peaking, but instead of collapsing onto the couch, you lace up your sneakers and step outside for a jog. This isn't just about burning calories; it's about fortifying the mind, building that emotional resilience every dad needs.

First off, let's talk about understanding the mind-body connection. Believe it or not, there's a treasure trove of scientific evidence supporting the idea that physical exercise can dramatically improve mood and reduce anxiety. Think of it as a natural mood enhancer, like sunlight after a dreary day. When you engage in physical activities, your brain releases endorphins— those feel-good chemicals that elevate your mood and help mitigate feelings of depression and anxiety. Exercise also promotes the production of neurotransmitters such as serotonin and norepinephrine, which play a critical role in regulating mood and combating stress.

Beyond chemistry, regular exercise builds a sense of accomplishment and control. Every mile you run or push-up you complete adds to your stockpile of small victories, creating a positive feedback loop that can combat daily stressors. Engaging in movement tells your brain that you're taking action, which can be incredibly empowering when life feels chaotic.

But how do you make sure this newfound knowledge translates into practical benefits? For many busy dads, finding time for exercise may seem like just one more thing to add to your plate. The trick lies in incorporating simple, effective activities into your routine without feeling like you're adding another chore to your list.

Here are some practical exercise tips. Start small. You don't need to transform into a marathon runner overnight. Begin with activities that fit seamlessly into your day. How about walking? It's a great low-impact exercise that requires no special equipment. You can even turn it into a social event by walking with your kids or a friend. Walking through the park, observing nature, and engaging in light conversation can be both refreshing and therapeutic.

Then there's biking. Dust off that old two-wheeler and take a ride around the neighborhood. Biking is not only good for your legs and cardiovascular health, but it's also a fun way to explore your surroundings. If you have children, they're often more than willing to join in, turning exercise into quality family time.

Don't forget about sports. Whether it's shooting hoops, throwing a frisbee, or kicking around a soccer ball, sports provide an excellent workout disguised as fun. Even if you're not an athlete, these activities encourage movement and engagement, giving you that much-needed break from routine stress.

Finding accountability is crucial to maintaining your exercise regimen. Let's face it, sticking to a workout plan can be tough, especially when life throws curveballs. Here's where having a support system makes all the difference. Consider enlisting a workout buddy. A friend or fellow dad who shares similar fitness goals can be a powerful motivator. Knowing you have someone counting on you can make it harder to skip that morning run or evening bike ride.

Fitness classes offer another layer of accountability. Whether it's a local gym class, a community center offering yoga, or a boot camp session in the park, the structured environment and scheduled times create a commitment you're less likely to break. Plus, being surrounded by others with similar fitness goals can be encouraging.

For the tech-savvy, fitness-focused apps may hit the spot. Apps like Strava, MyFitnessPal, or Nike Training Club provide guided workouts, track progress, and offer virtual communities. They can serve as both a motivator and a log of your journey, showing how far you've come and inspiring you to keep going.

Lastly, let's address using exercise as a stress relief tool. Physical activity becomes a powerful outlet for tension and frustration. When stress skyrockets, instead of internalizing it or lashing out, channel that energy into movement. There's something almost magical about pounding the pavement during a run or hitting a punching bag—it allows the physical release of pent-up stress.

Imagine this: after a heated phone call or a rough day, instead of sitting and stewing, you head to the gym or grab those running shoes. As you move, feel the rhythm of your breath and the steady beat of your heart. Each step, each punch, each stretch helps siphon off the negative energy, leaving you clear-headed and more grounded.

Incorporate moments of mindfulness into your workouts. Pay attention to the sensations in your body—the stretch in your muscles, the air filling your lungs, the ground beneath your feet. This focus not only improves the quality of your exercise but also serves as a meditative practice, helping to stabilize your emotions.

Adopting Relaxation Techniques like Meditation
When you're a divorced father, dealing with daily stress and emotional upheaval can feel like treading water in a stormy sea. Finding ways to build emotional resilience is crucial for not just surviving but thriving in this new chapter of life. One effective strategy is learning relaxation techniques that can mitigate stress and usher in a sense of peace. Let's dive into some practical methods to achieve this.

What is Meditation?

Meditation is often seen as the ultimate relaxation technique, but what exactly is it? It involves training the mind to grow more aware and focused, ultimately leading to a state of mental clarity, calmness, and emotional balance. Different forms of meditation cater to various needs and preferences. For instance, guided meditation involves following along with an instructor, either through audio recordings or in-person sessions. This can be a great starting point if you find it hard to concentrate on your own.

Mindfulness meditation, on the other hand, revolves around being present in the moment without judgment. It might sound simple, but it can be challenging in our distraction-filled lives. The benefits, however, are substantial: reduced anxiety, improved concentration, and better emotional health. Then there's transcendental meditation, which typically involves silently repeating a mantra to help settle the mind. Studies show that this type of meditation can lower blood pressure and reduce symptoms of Post Traumatic Stress Syndrome or PTSD.

Easy Meditation Practices

Getting started with meditation doesn't require a complete lifestyle overhaul. Here are some easy steps to begin meditating at home:

Choose Your Spot: Pick a quiet place where you won't be disturbed. Sit comfortably with your back straight, whether on a chair or a cushion on the floor.

Set a Timer: Start small for just 5-10 minutes. Use apps like Headspace or Calm, which offer guided sessions perfect for beginners.

Focus on Your Breath: Close your eyes and take deep breaths. Notice the sensation of the air entering and leaving your nostrils. If your mind wanders, gently bring it back to your breath.

Use Mantras or Guided Sessions: Repeat a calming word or phrase or listen to a guided session if that helps you stay focused.

These steps can be easily integrated into your day, perhaps in the morning before the household wakes up or at night to unwind. While it may feel awkward initially, consistency is key. Over time, meditation becomes a sanctuary for your mind amidst the chaos.

Creating a Relaxation Space

Your environment plays a significant role in how effectively you can relax and meditate. Creating a dedicated relaxation space at home can make a big difference. You don't need an entire room; even a corner will do. Here are some tips to set up your perfect relaxation zone:

Lighting: opt for soft, ambient lighting. Avoid harsh lights that strain your eyes and opt for candles or dimmable lamps instead.

Comfortable Seating: Choose something comfortable yet supportive. A cushioned chair or a yoga mat with pillows can work well.

Personal Touches: Incorporate elements that bring you peace—plants, soothing artworks, or family photos. These personal touches add a layer of comfort.

Sound: Play calming background music or nature sounds. Some apps provide tranquil soundscapes to enhance your meditation experience.

Aroma: Essential oils like lavender, eucalyptus, or sandalwood can create a calming atmosphere. Consider using a diffuser to spread these relaxing aromas.

Having a designated space signals to your brain that it's time to relax the same way climbing into bed tells your body it's time to sleep.

Integrating Meditation into Daily Life

Incorporating meditation into your daily routine is essential to reap its full benefits. Consistency and commitment are necessary, but they don't have to be burdensome tasks. Here are some strategies to seamlessly integrate meditation into your everyday life:

Morning Routine: Start your day with a short meditation session. This sets a positive tone and equips you to handle stress more effectively.

Work Breaks: Take mini meditation breaks during the workday. Even a few minutes of focusing on your breath can recharge your mind.

Evening Wind Down: Use evening meditation to clear your mind and prepare for a restful night's sleep.

Involve the Kids: Make meditation a family activity. Teach your children simple breathing exercises, turning it into quality time together while instilling good habits in them.

Track Progress: Use a journal or apps to track your progress. Seeing your improvements can be incredibly motivating.

By weaving meditation into your daily life, it shifts from being just another task on your to-do list to a natural part of your routine. Whether it's a challenging co-parenting situation, a demanding job, or the stress of re-entering the dating scene, meditation can help you tackle these challenges with a calmer, clearer mind.

Final Thoughts

As we draw this chapter to a close, it's clear that building emotional resilience as a divorced father is no small feat. By weaving mindfulness and self-care into your daily routine, you're giving yourself the tools to handle life's curveballs. Whether it's taking deep breaths during a stressful moment or unwinding with a good book at the end of the day, these practices will help you stay grounded and present.

Remember, it's not just about tackling stress head-on but also creating an environment that supports your well-being. Reframing negative thoughts, setting boundaries, and surrounding yourself with positive influences are all crucial steps to keep your emotional tank full. With these strategies in place, you'll find yourself better equipped to navigate the ups and downs of single fatherhood, emerging stronger and more resilient for both you and your kids.

SIX
Fostering Emotional Intelligence in Your Children

Fostering emotional intelligence in your children is like planting a garden. It requires patience, the right tools, and sometimes, a little extra watering to help those tender seedlings grow strong. Picture this: you're at a park watching your child navigate the social jungle gym of friendships and playground politics. Suddenly, someone doesn't share a toy, and emotions flare up faster than you can say "time-out." This chapter is all about equipping your little ones with the essential emotional skills they need to handle such moments gracefully, turning potential tantrums into opportunities for growth.

In this chapter, we'll explore the importance of creating an environment where open and honest communication thrives. You'll learn how to become an active listener—not just nodding and smiling but genuinely tuning in and engaging. We'll dive into the art of setting up safe spaces for discussions, making even the quirkiest mishaps (like gluing fingers together during crafts) a topic worth discussing. Moreover, you'll discover how modeling openness and sharing your own feelings can turn you into a superhero of emotional transparency. And let's not forget the regular check-ins – think of them as emotional weather reports that help your child become fluent in expressing their inner world. Get ready to cultivate a thriving garden of emotional intelligence, one heartfelt conversation at a time!

Encouraging Open and Honest Communication

Imagine building a model car with your child. You have all the pieces, the glue, and the instructions sprawled out. Now, think of fostering emotional intelligence as assembling that car—a little patience, a lot of understanding, and sometimes, extra glue to keep things together. In this section, we'll emphasize how to create an environment where children feel safe expressing their thoughts and feelings, which is essential for enhancing their emotional fluency.

Active Listening Skills

First off, let's talk about active listening. It's more than just nodding while your child talks about the latest playground drama. Active listening involves really tuning in, paraphrasing what they've said, and asking thoughtful questions. When your child tells you about their day, listen without interrupting. Reflect back what they say with phrases like, "So, you're feeling upset because your friend didn't share today?" This shows them you're engaged and validates their emotions. Asking open-ended questions like, "What do you think made your friend act that way?" can deepen their understanding and empathy. Essentially, active listening is the foundation upon which emotional fluency is built.

Creating Safe Spaces for Discussion

Now, let's move on to creating times and places for open conversations. Just like scheduling a playdate, it's important to designate moments when your child knows they can talk to you about anything—yes, even the time they accidentally glued their fingers together trying to make artwork. Perhaps during bedtime or during a weekly "family chat" on Sunday afternoons. The key here is consistency; these scheduled talks can become rituals your child looks forward to. During these times, stress that no topic is off-limits. Whether it's school worries or pondering why broccoli is green, encouraging openness means they'll come to you with the bigger stuff, too.

Modeling Openness

Next, let's chat about modeling openness. Think of yourself as the superhero of emotional transparency. Share your own feelings and experiences with your child, appropriately tailored to their age, of course. If you're stressed about work, you might say, "I'm feeling a bit overwhelmed with my job today, but talking about it helps." By being honest about your emotions, you show them that it's okay to have complex feelings and that expressing them isn't a sign of weakness but a strength. Your openness provides a roadmap for them to follow, making the human experience of emotions a shared journey instead of a solitary expedition.

Regular Check-Ins

Last but certainly not least, incorporate rituals like daily or weekly emotional status updates. Imagine it as a quick weather report but for feelings: "Today I'm feeling sunny with a chance of rain clouds around that math test." Normalize these expressions by making them regular events. For instance, during family dinners, everyone takes a turn sharing one good thing and one challenging thing about their day. This practice helps embed emotional expression into their routine, demystifying it and making it as normal as discussing their favorite cartoon.

Helping Them Express Their Emotions Positively

Teaching children various methods to convey their emotions constructively is a vital component of fostering healthier social interactions. This journey begins with helping them recognize and accurately label their feelings. Imagine you're at a family dinner, and your child suddenly bursts into tears. Instead of simply comforting them, guiding them through identifying what they're feeling is the first step towards emotional intelligence.

You can achieve this by using emotion charts, activities, and drawing or writing about their feelings. Emotion charts are visual tools that display different faces illustrating emotions like happiness, sadness, anger, and surprise. Have them point to the face that matches their current feeling. A practical activity is to ask them to draw what they feel inside. Maybe it's a stormy sky for anger or a sunny day for happiness. Another activity could involve storytelling where they write about their day, focusing on moments that triggered specific emotions. By doing this regularly, they're more likely to understand the subtleties between feeling sad and feeling lonely, for instance.

Next, guide them in using constructive language to express those feelings. Instead of vague and often unhelpful statements like 'I'm mad,' encourage them to be specific — 'I feel frustrated because my tower keeps falling.' This practice not only helps them articulate their needs but also provides others with clear insight into how they can offer support. Role-playing scenarios are incredibly beneficial here. Play out different situations where they practice using "I feel" statements. For instance, if they're upset about sharing toys, role-play a scene where they say, "I feel upset when I don't get a turn because I enjoy playing with that toy too."

Creative outlets such as art, music, sports, and journaling offer another powerful avenue for emotional expression. Encourage your child to participate in activities they enjoy, whether it's painting, playing the piano, or dribbling a basketball. These activities serve as a dual purpose: they provide an outlet for pent-up emotions and foster a sense of achievement and self-worth. For example, sketching can be a therapeutic exercise where children pour their emotions onto a blank canvass, creating something beautiful from their complex feelings. Similarly, sports can act as a physical release, where running or swimming helps them burn off stress and frustration. Journaling, another excellent outlet, allows them to reflect on their experiences and emotions, providing both clarity and relief.

Incorporating mindfulness tools like deep breathing exercises and grounding techniques into their routine can also make a significant difference. Mindfulness is all about bringing one's attention to the present moment, which is crucial during emotionally charged situations. Teach your child simple deep breathing exercises such as the "4-7-8" technique: inhaling for four seconds, holding the breath for seven seconds, and exhaling slowly for eight seconds. Make it a fun activity by pretending to blow up a giant balloon or imagine they're a dragon breathing out fire. Grounding techniques, such as focusing on five things they can see, four things they can touch, three things they can hear, two things they can smell, and one thing they can taste, can also help stabilize them during emotional upheavals.

While fostering these skills, it's essential to maintain a supportive and understanding environment. Children thrive when they know they are heard and their emotions are validated. Avoid dismissive phrases like "Stop crying" or "Don't be silly." Instead, acknowledge their feelings with comments like, "I see you're feeling really upset right now. Let's talk about it." This validation helps build trust and encourages them to share their emotions openly without fear of judgment or reprimand.

Additionally, consider establishing a daily check-in ritual where everyone shares one high and one low from their day. This not only normalizes talking about emotions but also helps children learn that experiencing a range of emotions is a natural part of life. By modeling this behavior yourself, you show them that even adults deal with complex emotions and that there's no shame in expressing what's going on inside.

Another effective strategy is to create a calm-down corner in your home. This space should be filled with comforting items like soft cushions, sensory objects, or calming music. When your child feels overwhelmed, guide them to this area where they can engage in deep breathing or listen to soothing sounds until they feel ready to communicate their feelings more clearly. Knowing they have a safe space to retreat to when things get intense can significantly reduce anxiety and promote emotional regulation.

As children grow, their emotional vocabulary and regulation strategies should evolve with them. Reinforce positive behavior by celebrating small victories. If your child successfully uses an "I feel" statement during a conflict, acknowledge it with praise, "I noticed you said 'I feel' instead of getting angry. That's awesome!" Such recognition reinforces their efforts and motivates them to continue practicing these skills.

Teaching Empathy and Understanding

Empathy is a cornerstone of emotional intelligence and an essential skill for fostering meaningful connections. As fathers, instilling the ability to empathize in your children can profoundly impact their relationships with peers and family members. Here's how you can start this journey by engaging them in activities that nurture empathy.

Begin with role-playing. Role-playing scenarios allow children to step into someone else's shoes and experience different perspectives. Create situations where they have to consider how a character might feel and react. For instance, you could act out a scene where one child feels left out during a game. Ask your child to be the one who includes the excluded child, discussing afterward how each role felt. This simple exercise not only builds empathy but also encourages children to practice inclusion and kindness actively.

Another powerful method is to discuss literature or movie characters' motivations. Stories offer a treasure trove of opportunities to explore emotions and viewpoints. When reading a book or watching a film, pause occasionally to ask questions like, "Why do you think this character acted this way?" or "How would you feel if you were in their situation?" For example, books like "Charlotte's Web" by E.B. White provide rich material to discuss themes of friendship and sacrifice. Relating to fictional characters allows children to understand complex emotions in a safe and controlled environment.

Frequent discussions about the emotional experiences of others further reinforce empathy. Share personal stories from your own life where empathy played a role. Describe a time when you misunderstood someone's feelings and what you learned from it. Encourage your children to talk about their day, focusing on the emotions they observed in themselves and others. These conversations make empathy a regular part of their thought process, helping them relate better to the emotions of those around them.

Understanding nonverbal cues is another critical aspect of empathy-building. Teach your children to read body language through interactive activities. For instance, play a game where each person takes turns expressing different emotions without using words, while others guess the emotion. Discuss how facial expressions, posture, and gestures convey feelings. Highlighting these subtle signals helps children become more attuned to the unspoken emotions of others. Use everyday moments as teachable instances; if you notice a friend appearing downcast, point it out and discuss possible reasons and ways to approach them sensitively.

Next, foster problem-solving skills with an emphasis on considering others' feelings. Present various scenarios where conflicts arise and guide your children in brainstorming empathetic solutions. For example, describe a situation where friends argue over a toy. Ask your child how each party might feel and what steps could resolve the conflict while acknowledging everyone's emotions. Encourage them to come up with multiple solutions and discuss the potential outcomes of each. This practice not only enhances problem-solving abilities but also ingrains the importance of empathy in conflict resolution.

To wrap things up, there are several guidelines you can implement to systematically build empathy:

Role-Playing: Set aside time regularly for role-playing different social situations. Create a range of scenarios from common schoolyard issues to more complex family dynamics. Discuss and reflect on the emotions experienced during these exercises.

Literature and Movies: Incorporate books and films known for strong character development and emotional depth into your routine. Use these mediums as springboards for deeper conversations about motivation, feelings, and moral dilemmas.

Discuss Emotional Experiences: Make it a habit to discuss daily emotional encounters. Whether it's something that happened at school or within the family, use these moments to explore emotions and perspectives together.

Read Body Language: Practice identifying and interpreting body language through games and daily observations. Encourage children to be mindful of nonverbal cues and discuss what different postures or expressions might signify.

Scenario-Based Problem Solving: Introduce hypothetical scenarios regularly. Engage in discussions about how different solutions might affect others emotionally. Reinforce the idea that understanding and addressing emotions is key to resolving conflicts.

By integrating these activities and techniques into your parenting, you'll help your children cultivate a deep sense of empathy. They'll develop the ability to connect emotionally with others, reflecting positively on their interactions and relationships throughout their lives. Remember, empathy is not just a single lesson but a continuous practice. Through consistent effort and engagement, you'll see your children grow into compassionate individuals capable of forming strong emotional bonds with those around them.

Recognizing and Addressing Behavioral Issues Early

Identifying emotional disturbances and behavioral problems early in children is vital for providing the necessary interventions. As a dad navigating the complexities of co-parenting, dating, and being a role model, it's crucial to be vigilant about your child's emotional well-being.

First off, monitoring changes in behavior and social interactions can serve as an early alert system for emotional distress. Imagine your child suddenly becomes withdrawn or more aggressive. These behavior shifts can indicate underlying issues like anxiety or depression. Keep an eye on how they interact with friends and family. Are they isolating themselves? Do they frequently lash out? If you notice these signs, don't dismiss them as "just a phase." Instead, take a moment to dig deeper and understand the root cause.

Next up is working together on strategies and action plans to address concerns as they arise. Picture this: You spot some troubling behavior in your child. What next? Sit down with them and have a heart-to-heart.

Constructive dialogues can go a long way in understanding what's going on in their minds. Together, you can build a doable action plan that includes simple steps like setting routines, identifying triggers, and finding calming activities. It's all about creating a team effort where the child feels involved and supported.

Now, let's talk about seeking professional help when needed. There's no denying it—sometimes, dads need backup. Discussing the importance of professional help openly can normalize therapy as a strength rather than a weakness. Imagine telling your child, "It's okay to see a therapist; they can help you work through your feelings, just like a coach helps you with sports." This approach removes the stigma and encourages your child to view therapy as another tool in their emotional toolkit.

Creating an environment that promotes positive behaviors is another critical step. Think about setting up a reward system for achievements, no matter how small. Did your child use words instead of fists during a disagreement? Celebrate it! Consistent positive reinforcement can boost their self-esteem and encourage more of the same good behavior. It's like giving a high-five for each win, big or small.

When it comes to vigilance, don't underestimate the power of consistency. Regularly check in with your child and observe any patterns in their behavior. Maybe they're more anxious before school, or perhaps they seem sad after visiting a friend. Keeping track of these moments over time can provide valuable insights into what might be causing their emotional turmoil.

In fostering constructive dialogues, remember that timing and setting matter. Choose a calm, quiet environment where your child feels safe to open up. Avoid jumping straight into solutions; first, listen actively. Paraphrase their words: "I hear you're feeling upset because..." This shows empathy and validates their emotions, making them more likely to engage in problem-solving discussions.

Normalizing therapy doesn't stop at just talking about it. Lead by example if you can. Share stories of people who've benefited from professional help or discuss your own experiences with counseling. Make therapy part of the routine conversation, not a taboo topic. When your child sees therapy as a normal and beneficial experience, they're more likely to accept and embrace it.

Positive reinforcement should be balanced and genuine. It's not about giving trophies for every task accomplished but recognizing efforts that align with positive behavior. For instance, praise them for practicing patience or showing kindness. Create a "celebration jar" where they can add notes about their achievements, and occasionally review these milestones together. This practice fosters a sense of accomplishment and resilience.

Stories and examples resonate deeply with children. Use relatable tales to explain complex emotions and coping mechanisms. For instance, share how a character from their favorite story dealt with sadness or anger. Relatability can demystify emotions and offer comforting proof that everyone struggles sometimes and that it's okay to seek help.

Regular family meetings can also serve as a platform for open dialogue and collective strategizing. Designate a weekly time where everyone checks in emotionally. Use this session to discuss any behavioral changes or introduce new strategies for managing emotions. Establishing this routine can make conversations about feelings more natural and less intimidating.

Introducing mindfulness practices can be another effective strategy within your action plan. Simple exercises like deep breathing or guided imagery can help children manage stress and anxiety. Practice these techniques together; turn it into a fun bonding activity. Moreover, integrating mindfulness into daily routines can equip them with lifelong tools for emotional regulation.

Encouraging artistic expression is another powerful tool. Art, music, and writing can be therapeutic outlets for children to process and express their emotions. Set aside creative time where you both engage in drawing, painting, or journaling. This not only provides an emotional outlet but also strengthens your bond.

Finally, maintaining an open line of communication with educators and caregivers is essential. They often spend significant time with your child and can provide useful insights into their behavior patterns and emotional state. Collaborate with them to ensure a cohesive support system for your child both at home and outside.

Closing Remarks

We've covered a lot of ground in this chapter, from actively listening to our kids' daily dramas to setting up those sacred, no-judgment "talk times." It's kind of like being their emotional handyman, always ready with a toolbox full of empathetic responses and thoughtful questions. By creating safe spaces for your children to share, modeling openness yourself, and making check-ins a regular thing, you're helping them build the sturdy framework they need for emotional intelligence. Remember, it's about consistency, patience, and sometimes, a bit of creativity (like pretending to blow up that giant balloon while practicing deep breathing).

As we wrap things up, just think of all these strategies as unique pieces of a puzzle that, when put together, create a clearer picture of emotionally resilient kids. Encouraging positive ways for them to express emotions, teaching empathy through everyday moments and role-playing, and recognizing early signs of behavioral issues will make a world of difference. This journey is all about connection and understanding, helping your child navigate the maze of feelings with confidence and kindness. And hey, it also means fewer glued-together fingers and more emotionally secure kiddos!

SEVEN
Navigating Legal and Custody Battles

Navigating legal and custody battles as a divorced father can feel like you've just stepped into a courtroom drama or reality television show. The stakes are high, the rules confusing, and the whole ordeal is stressful enough to turn your hair gray overnight (if it isn't already). But fear not! This chapter will arm you with the essential knowledge and strategies you need to become a veritable ninja in the legal dojo. You'll soon transform from a bewildered dad fumbling through paperwork to a confident advocate for your children's welfare, prepared to face any courtroom challenge with poise and determination.

DISCLAIMER: This book should not be utilized as legal consultation. Each state and situation are different, and I highly encourage you to utilize the assistance of an experienced attorney if you can afford one. There are also countless legal resources in your local family courts to guide you through the process if you feel lost or confused. Don't be afraid to use them and to educate yourself in your unique circumstances.

In this chapter, we'll explore the tangled web of legal jargon and custody terms that often leave fathers feeling more perplexed than a cat in a dog show. We'll start by demystifying your rights concerning custody and visitation, so you'll know exactly what you're entitled to when it comes to parenting time and decision-making.

Next, we'll delve into the importance of understanding jurisdictional differences in custody laws—because what flies in Texas might crash and burn in California. Moreover, you'll discover the significance of gathering credible information and meticulous documentation to bolster your case. By the end of this chapter, you'll be equipped with tips on finding valuable resources and professional guidance to help navigate the legal maze, turning intimidating legal proceedings into manageable tasks. So, buckle up and get ready to conquer the legal system like the super dad you are!

Understanding Your Legal Rights as a Father

Navigating the turbulent waters of divorce and custody battles can be daunting for anyone, but it's especially challenging for fathers. Understanding your legal rights isn't just about protecting yourself; it's also about securing your children's welfare. This section aims to arm you with the knowledge and tools to advocate effectively for your interests and those of your children.

First and foremost, know your rights regarding custody, visitation, and involvement in your children's lives. It's crucial to grasp these rights so you can stand firm when advocating for yourself in court or during mediation. Custody, for instance, is often divided into two categories: legal and physical. Legal custody refers to the right to make important decisions about your child's upbringing, such as their education, health care, and religious training. Physical custody, on the other hand, pertains to where the child will live. You might have joint custody, offering shared responsibilities and time with the child, or sole custody, where one parent takes on the majority of responsibilities.

Understanding these distinctions is vital because they define how much influence you can have in your child's life post-divorce. Poor knowledge of your rights may lead you to inadvertently give up more than you should during negotiations, limiting your role in your child's life. Familiarize yourself with common terms and concepts related to custody and visitation through reliable online resources and informational guides. These can provide a solid foundation for discussions with legal professionals and help you approach your case with confidence.

Next, it's essential to be aware that custody and parenting rights can vary significantly by jurisdiction. States have different laws and regulations governing divorce and child custody cases, which means what applies in one state may not apply in another. For example, some states have a preference for joint custody arrangements, while others might lean towards awarding sole custody based on various factors. Knowing the specifics of your jurisdiction will allow you to tailor your strategy accordingly. Researching local laws or consulting with a family law attorney who specializes in your area can provide clarity and direction. Not only does this knowledge prepare you for legal proceedings, but it also reduces surprises that could derail your case.

To navigate these differences effectively, access to credible information is indispensable. Online databases and local organizations dedicated to fathers' rights are valuable resources. Websites like Civil eCourts Access offer accessible portals for legal documents and case records, helping you understand the procedural aspects of your case. Additionally, local community centers often host workshops and seminars that focus on fathers' rights and provide guidance on navigating the legal system. These resources can be lifesavers, offering both educational content and emotional support from people who have faced similar challenges.

When armed with knowledge about your rights and the specific laws of your jurisdiction, you're better prepared to confront any legal challenges head-on. However, knowing what to do when your rights are compromised is equally critical. Meticulously documenting incidents if your legal rights are violated can serve as invaluable evidence during legal proceedings. For instance, if your ex denies you visitation rights or makes unilateral decisions impacting your child, keep detailed records of these incidents. Note dates, times, descriptions of events, and even collect screenshots or emails that corroborate your claims.

Such documentation is not just a precaution—it's a necessity when preparing for discussions with your lawyer or presenting your case in court. Courts tend to favor well-documented cases supported by tangible evidence, so having a thorough record can significantly strengthen your position. Consult with your attorney on the best ways to document these incidents to ensure your records meet legal standards and can be effectively utilized when needed.

Finding the Right Legal Representation
Navigating Legal and Custody Battles: Choosing the Right Attorney

When you're caught in the whirlwind of a divorce or custody battle, having a competent legal representative by your side can make all the difference. This section is designed to help you, as a father, understand the importance of securing skilled legal representation and how to choose the best attorney for your needs.

Let's start with the basics: qualifications and experience. Finding an attorney who specializes in family law is crucial. Why? Because family law is a complex field that requires specific knowledge and proficiency. Think of it this way: you wouldn't go to a general practitioner for heart surgery, right? Similarly, you shouldn't rely on a lawyer who doesn't focus on family law. Look for attorneys who have solid experience handling cases similar to yours. Their know-how in navigating the intricacies of family law will greatly benefit your case. For instance, an attorney experienced in child custody issues would be better equipped to present your case compellingly.

Interviewing potential attorneys is another critical step. Asking key questions during initial consultations will give you valuable insights. Start with basic inquiries about their experience and success rates in family law cases. Dive deeper into specifics like their approach to handling your type of situation, mediation training, and courtroom track record. Don't forget to ask about their fee structure and if they offer alternative payment arrangements. But remember, it's not just about the questions you ask—it's also about how they respond. Are they attentive? Do they explain things clearly? These factors are important as they indicate how well they might handle your case.

Understanding the potential costs involved with legal representation is essential to avoid any financial surprises down the road. Legal fees can quickly add up, so it's vital to have a clear picture of what to expect. During your consultations, make sure to discuss the attorney's billing practices. Some lawyers charge by the hour, while others may offer flat rate fees for specific services. If you're on a tight budget, inquire about the possibility of alternative fee arrangements. It's also worth asking about any additional costs that might arise, such as filing fees or charges for administrative support. By understanding these details upfront, you can plan accordingly and avoid financial stress later.

Building a trusting relationship with your attorney is fundamental to making the legal process smoother and less stressful. Effective communication is the cornerstone of this relationship. Ensure you feel comfortable discussing personal matters with your attorney, as openness and honesty will help them represent you better. Establish clear channels for communication from the get-go. Ask how often you'll receive updates on your case and the preferred mode of communication—whether through phone calls, emails, or in-person meetings. Consistent and transparent communication will help you stay informed and engaged throughout the legal proceedings.

Let's shift focus to the initial consultation with your potential attorney. This meeting is your opportunity to gauge their expertise and compatibility with your values. Treat it like a job interview but remember, they're applying to work for you. Observe their demeanor. Are they rushed, or do they take the time to listen and understand your concerns? A good attorney should make you feel heard and supported. Also, consider their dedication to your case. An attorney who shows genuine interest and empathy is likely to be more committed to achieving the best possible outcome for you.

Think about the long-term relationship you're about to establish. Legal battles, especially those involving custody, can be lengthy. You need an attorney who not only possesses the necessary legal skills but is also someone you can trust over time. Trust is built through consistent actions—like returning your calls promptly and keeping you updated on any developments in your case. If at any point you feel uneasy or doubting the attorney's commitment, it's better to reconsider than to proceed with uncertainty.

For example, consider a father in Houston who ignored his attorney's advice about quitting drinking. He ended up losing significant custody rights and had his child support increased. This real-life scenario underscores the importance of following your legal counsel's guidance. They are there to protect your interests and ensure you present yourself in the best possible light in court.

While costs are inevitable, they shouldn't come as a surprise. Clear communication about fee structures helps you budget effectively. Hourly rates can vary significantly among attorneys, so understanding the billing process is crucial. Ask for a detailed breakdown of potential costs, including any hidden fees. Being financially prepared can alleviate one aspect of the stress associated with legal battles.

A practical tip is to keep a detailed record of all interactions and agreements with your attorney. It can be as simple as maintaining a journal where you note down the dates and key points discussed during each meeting or phone call. This record-keeping helps in maintaining transparency and ensures that both parties are on the same page regarding expectations and responsibilities.

Humor can be a great way to ease into building rapport with your attorney. While it's a serious matter, light-hearted conversation at appropriate times can help create a comfortable atmosphere. After all, you're working together towards a common goal, and establishing a friendly relationship can make the journey less daunting.

Lastly, always trust your instincts. If you feel confident and comfortable with an attorney during the initial consultation, that's a positive sign. On the other hand, if you have reservations, don't hesitate to explore other options. Remember, this decision is crucial for your future and your relationship with your children.

In conclusion, securing a competent family law attorney involves thorough research, asking the right questions, understanding the costs, and building a trusting relationship. Take your time to find someone who meets your legal needs and aligns with your values. Your choice of attorney can significantly impact the outcome of your case, so choose wisely and confidently.

Preparing for Custody Hearings and Negotiations

Navigating the legal landscape of custody hearings can be daunting for divorced fathers. Equipping yourself with the right tools and strategies can make all the difference in achieving a favorable outcome. In this section, we will explore various methods to prepare effectively for custody hearings and negotiations.

First and foremost, gathering documentation that demonstrates your involvement in your children's lives is paramount. This includes school reports, medical records, and evidence of participation in extracurricular activities. Creating a parenting time calendar can be especially beneficial. It details the specific dates, times, and locations for child exchanges, which helps minimize confusion and reduces conflicts. Not only does it provide clear, factual evidence of your involvement, but it also promotes consistency and stability for your child. Maintaining such detailed records can significantly bolster your case.

Documentation doesn't end once an agreement is reached. Continue maintaining detailed records even after reaching a custody agreement. Ongoing documentation supports effective co-parenting, helps monitor compliance with the agreement, and ensures you are prepared for any future mediation or legal proceedings, such as modifications or appeals. Remember, whether you're seeking primary custody, joint custody, or modifying an existing arrangement, the strength of your case often relies on the detailed records you maintain.

Next, understanding typical courtroom procedures is crucial. Familiarizing yourself with the flow of the trial can greatly reduce stress and enable you to present your case confidently. A custody trial typically begins with opening statements, followed by the presentation of evidence through witness testimonies and documentary exhibits. Knowing what to expect at each stage can help you remain composed and focused. For instance, when presenting your case, it's essential to have all your documents printed and numbered in advance. Bring multiple copies for the judge, opposing counsel, and yourself.

Effective communication is another critical aspect of preparing for custody hearings. Practicing clear and concise communication can minimize misunderstandings and enhance negotiation outcomes. When communicating with the court and other parties involved, always aim to be direct and to the point. Avoid using overly complex language or legal jargon. The goal is to ensure that your message is understood clearly and accurately. Don't allow emotional language, accusations, or insults to define your position in the case.

Role-playing scenarios is an excellent way to build confidence and anticipate potential opposing arguments. Practicing responses to potential questions from the opposing party or the judge allows you to refine your answers and reduce the chances of being caught off guard during the actual hearing. Develop a list of possible questions and rehearse your responses with a trusted friend or family member. This exercise can help you feel more prepared and less nervous when it's time to present your case.

Furthermore, consulting with professionals can be invaluable. Working with a family law attorney can ensure that your documentation meets legal standards and effectively supports your case. Additionally, consider consulting a mediator or child custody evaluator for further insights into strengthening your case. These professionals can provide guidance on how to best present your evidence and what types of documentation will be most persuasive.

When it comes to gathering evidence, remember that it can come in many forms. Official documents, school records, personal records, text message screenshots, emails, photographs, and videos are all valuable pieces of evidence. These items can provide a snapshot of the dynamics between you and the other parent and offer insights into your child's well-being. For example, text messages and emails can document interactions and demonstrate your ongoing involvement in your child's life.

It's not just about collecting evidence though; it's about building a narrative around your child's best interests. A well-maintained record of your interactions with the other parent and your child can significantly strengthen your case. Utilize apps like Our Family Wizard, AppClose, or Talking Parents to manage and document communications. If you don't use a co-parenting app, create a separate log that documents and provides a timeline for all communications between you and the other parent.

Selecting and preparing witnesses is another key component in strengthening your case. Witnesses can corroborate your claims and provide a third-party perspective on your interactions with your child. They can be professionals like teachers or daycare providers who have had frequent contact with your child, or friends and other parents who have observed your interactions. Clearly inform your witnesses about the purpose of their testimony, practice questioning with them, and emphasize honesty. This preparation can help them provide credible and effective testimonies.

Finally, always maintain a high standard of behavior during court proceedings. How you conduct yourself can influence the judge's perception of you as a parent. Behave professionally and avoid any actions that could be perceived as childish or uncooperative. Judges often take cues from your courtroom demeanor to gauge how you might behave outside of court.

Dealing with Child Support and Alimony Issues

Navigating the intricacies of child support and alimony is a significant challenge for many divorced fathers. Understanding these financial obligations can provide you with the confidence needed to manage them effectively. Be aware that not all situations warrant the need for a father to pay child support. Knowing how child support is determined and calculated is essential. Contrary to popular belief, there are moms who pay child support to the father in some cases. Know your rights and obligations in detail.

First, let's dive into how child support is calculated and the role of alimony. Child support calculations typically consider factors like the income of both parents, the number of children, and the time each parent spends with the children. The idea is to ensure that the children's needs are met adequately and fairly. Alimony, on the other hand, serves to support a spouse who may have been financially dependent during the marriage. It considers factors such as the length of the marriage, the recipient's earning capacity, and the lifestyle maintained during the marriage.

Gathering comprehensive financial documentation is crucial in this process. This includes pay stubs, tax returns, bank statements, and any other relevant financial records. Having these documents ready and organized can establish your credibility and transparency during court hearings. Courts appreciate thoroughness and honesty, and presenting well-prepared financial information can significantly impact the decisions made regarding your support obligations.

If circumstances change, knowing how to request adjustments to support orders through proper channels becomes vital. Life is unpredictable—unemployment, medical emergencies, or other significant changes in circumstance are common. When your situation changes, petitioning the court for an alteration in the support order is necessary. This requires gathering evidence of the changed circumstances and filing the appropriate paperwork. It might seem daunting, but it ensures that the financial responsibilities reflect the current reality accurately.

Avoiding common pitfalls in these financial matters is also essential. Misunderstandings often arise from communication gaps or misinterpretations of one another's intentions. Drawing clear boundaries and encouraging open dialogues can help prevent these issues. For example, always communicate through official channels and document interactions to avoid disputes. Additionally, being proactive rather than reactive can save you from many headaches. If you foresee an issue, address it directly and early, rather than letting it fester.

Navigating child support and alimony doesn't have to be an insurmountable task. By understanding how obligations are calculated, gathering necessary documentation, knowing how to request modifications, and avoiding pitfalls, you can handle these responsibilities with greater ease and confidence. This approach not only benefits you but also ensures that your children's needs are prioritized in a fair and balanced manner, contributing to their overall well-being.

Bringing It All Together

Understanding the maze of legal rights and custody can feel overwhelmig, but it's doable with the right knowledge. We've tackled how crucial it is to know your rights inside out and the importance of documentation to back up your claims. Remember, ignorance isn't bliss when it comes to custody; it's more like jumping into quicksand. And knowing the specific laws in your state? That's like having the treasure map in a pirate adventure—crucial for finding the gold.

As we wrap things up, keep in mind that arming yourself with credible information and a strong attorney can make all these legal battles less daunting. Don't forget the power of meticulous record-keeping—your new best friend in this journey. By being proactive and prepared, you're not just protecting yourself; you're securing a brighter future for you and your kids. Now, take a deep breath, and let's get ready to tackle the next adventure, one step at a time.

EIGHT
Establishing New Family Traditions

Establishing new family traditions is a bit like deciding that Wednesdays are now officially "Wear Your Shirt Backwards Day"—a simple idea that can lead to hilarious photo ops and memorable moments. When it comes to reimagining holidays and special occasions after a divorce, creating unique celebrations not only brings joy but also fosters a sense of belonging within the newly formed family unit. Forget about replicating the past; the key here is to invent new quirks that everyone can look forward to, much like how a movie night with homemade popcorn always seems to make everything better.

In this chapter, we'll dive into a treasure trove of ideas for reinventing your family's holiday traditions. From whipping up legendary meals where everyone has a culinary role (yes, even if it's just stirring the pot!) to setting yearly themes that infuse each celebration with specific flavors—think "The Year of Adventure" or "The Year of Kindness." We'll also explore the invaluable input of your kids in shaping these traditions, proving that incorporating their creative suggestions can turn an ordinary New Year's Eve into a pajama-clad festival or transform Thanksgiving into a day of community service and charity runs. Whether through annual challenges, themed dinners, or documenting your journey in quirky scrapbooks and video diaries, this chapter will equip you with the tools to create new rituals that strengthen bonds and fill your home with laughter and love.

Celebrating Holidays and Special Occasions

Creating new family traditions around holidays can be a powerful way to foster connection and joy within your newly redefined family unit. Following a divorce, these unique celebrations can play a crucial role in nurturing a sense of belonging and shared happiness.

Creating Unique Family Holidays

Tailoring holidays to reflect your new family dynamics is essential. Forget about trying to duplicate past celebrations; instead, create something new that resonates with everyone involved. Consider starting with the holidays you already recognize and build upon them. For instance, transform Christmas into "Family Christmas" where each member contributes to its uniqueness, from making special ornaments together to creating quirky family-themed games.

One simple but effective tradition is cooking a special holiday meal as a family, with each person responsible for a different dish. This not only fosters teamwork but also allows everyone to bring something personal to the table – literally and figuratively. Make sure these meals become legendary by introducing annual recipe challenges or themed dinners, adding an element of anticipation and fun.

Incorporating Each Child's Input

Involving your children in creating these new traditions is vital. Allowing each child to share their favorite old traditions or suggest new ones promotes open communication and makes them feel valued. Maybe one child loves the idea of a family pajama day on New Year's Eve, while another is passionate about starting an annual charity run during Thanksgiving. Including their input helps form a cohesive, inclusive environment that caters to everyone's interests.

An effective way to gather ideas is through a "Family Tradition Meeting." Hold these meetings every few months where everyone can pitch their ideas. Use creative methods like drawing out ideas in a scrapbook, which not only makes the planning fun but serves as a visual reminder of everyone's contributions.

Yearly Goals or Themes

Setting yearly themes can add a layer of cohesion and excitement to your holiday celebrations. Imagine each year having a specific focus, such as "The Year of Adventure," dedicated to outdoor activities and travel-themed decorations, or "The Year of Kindness," focusing on community service projects and acts of kindness. These themes can inject creativity into your holidays and help build continuity from one year to the next.

To maintain enthusiasm throughout the year, create a family calendar marking when each themed activity will take place. Collaborate on this calendar at the beginning of the year, ensuring everyone has something to look forward to and contribute to. For example, if the theme is "The Year of Learning," plan museum visits, science experiments, or even a mini family TED Talk night where each person presents something they're passionate about.

Documenting Traditions

Documenting these new traditions helps preserve memories and creates a tangible narrative of your evolving family story. One effective method is keeping a family scrapbook where you paste pictures, ticket stubs, and written reflections from each event. This activity doesn't just record occasions but becomes an engaging tradition in itself, where everyone looks forward to adding their piece to the book after each celebration.

Another modern approach is creating a video diary. Dedicate time during each holiday to capture short video clips of what you're doing and how everyone feels about it. Over the years, these recordings will become priceless treasures that show how your family has grown and changed. Even setting up an annual photo booth corner with props related to your yearly theme can add an extra dose of fun and visual nostalgia.

Lastly, encouraging each family member to write a brief reflection or draw something representing their favorite part of the holiday fosters mindfulness and appreciation for these moments. These entries can be compiled into a digital family journal, making it easy to revisit these cherished memories anytime you wish.

Starting New Rituals for Weekends

Creating new family traditions can be a wonderful way to bring everyone closer after a divorce. One effective method is establishing positive routines that enhance togetherness during weekends. These activities serve as anchors, creating a sense of stability and belonging for both children and parents.

One such tradition is setting aside time for a Weekly Family Movie Night. Pick a consistent day and let everyone take turns choosing the film, ensuring there's something for all tastes. Engaging in shared entertainment allows families to relax and enjoy each other's company without distractions. Make it special with homemade popcorn, themed snacks, or even dressing up as characters from the movie. This not only provides quality time together but also opens up conversations about the stories and themes presented in the films, fostering deeper connections and understanding among family members. This routine can become a cherished part of your week, giving everyone something to look forward to and breaking the monotony of daily life.

Another great routine is planning Outdoor Adventures. Spending time in nature offers several benefits, including physical health and teamwork. Whether it's hiking, picnics, or simply exploring local parks, these outings encourage everyone to be active and work together. For example, navigating a hiking trail involves problem-solving and collaboration, building trust and communication skills within the family unit. It's also an excellent opportunity to teach children about nature, wildlife, and the importance of preserving the environment. The shared experiences and challenges faced during these adventures help strengthen family bonds, creating lasting memories and a sense of unity. Plus, being outdoors can have a calming effect, reducing stress and promoting overall wellness.

Cooking Together is another activity that can reinforce family ties. Set aside time on weekends to prepare meals as a family. Choose recipes that everyone can participate in, from simple dishes like homemade pizza to more complex ones that require teamwork. Cooking together teaches valuable life skills such as measuring ingredients, following instructions, and understanding nutrition. More importantly, it fosters a spirit of collaboration and mutual support. For instance, one person might handle chopping vegetables while another stirs the pot, exemplifying how working together leads to a delicious result. It's also a chance to share family recipes and cultural heritage, making mealtime a meaningful experience that connects generations.

A fun and educational tradition is designating a Skill-Sharing Day. Each week, allow a different family member to showcase a skill or hobby they are passionate about. This could range from drawing and playing musical instruments to coding or baking. Such activities foster appreciation for each other's talents and interests. For example, if one child is enthusiastic about photography, they can teach the family basic techniques and perhaps embark on a photo walk. This not only hones their skills but also invites others to appreciate and engage in what they love. Through these sessions, family members learn from one another and celebrate individual strengths, contributing to a supportive and encouraging home environment. This practice promotes self-esteem and mutual respect, as each person gets their moment to shine and demonstrate their unique abilities.

Incorporating these routines into your weekends can vastly improve family dynamics. Establishing new family traditions provides a much-needed structure and predictability, especially post-divorce when things can feel uncertain. These activities offer an escape from the usual stressors and create opportunities for genuine interaction, helping to rebuild trust and emotional connections.

To ensure the success of these traditions, involve everyone in the planning process. Ask for input on movie selections, outdoor destinations, and meal ideas. This inclusion makes each family member feel valued and invested in the activities. Additionally, be flexible and willing to adapt based on feedback. If a particular activity isn't resonating, brainstorm alternatives together. The goal is to find what works best for your unique family dynamic and to keep the experiences enjoyable and engaging for all.

Moreover, keep these routines light-hearted and fun. Use humor to make the time spent together more enjoyable. Laughing together over a funny movie scene, a cooking mishap, or a playful competition during a hike creates memorable moments and strengthens familial bonds. These shared jokes and light-hearted interactions become part of your family lore, making the new traditions even more special.

Establishing new family traditions through positive weekend routines does more than just fill time; it weaves a fabric of connection that can sustain and enrich your family's life. By making the effort to incorporate weekly movie nights, outdoor adventures, cooking sessions, and skill-sharing days, you're laying down the foundation for stronger relationships and treasured memories. These practices not only provide immediate joy and cohesion but also instill lifelong values and lessons in your children, helping them grow into well-rounded individuals who cherish family bonds.

Planning Family Vacations and Outings

Family adventures play a crucial role in creating lasting bonds and shared experiences, especially following a significant life change like divorce. One way to foster these connections is by establishing new family traditions that encourage togetherness and fun. Let's explore some practical ideas to help you build these meaningful moments.

Creating a Family Bucket List can become an exciting tradition that brings the entire family together. Start by gathering everyone around the table and brainstorming outings and vacations each member desires. This process is not only empowering for children, who get to voice their opinions, but it also serves as a roadmap for future plans. Imagine the thrill of checking off items on the list, whether it's visiting a new theme park, taking a hot air balloon ride, or exploring a historical site. By involving everyone, you ensure that the activities reflect the family's collective interests and aspirations, making each adventure more memorable and inclusive.

An Annual Camping Trip can be another delightful tradition that reinforces family unity. Camping offers unique opportunities for bonding through shared challenges and outdoor skills. From setting up tents to cooking meals over a campfire, every task becomes a team effort. Additionally, the natural setting provides a refreshing escape from daily routines and screens, allowing families to reconnect with one another more deeply. The simplicity of camping can help family members develop stronger communication skills and mutual reliance, which are essential for nurturing healthy relationships post-divorce. Plus, the sense of accomplishment derived from overcoming outdoor challenges can boost each person's confidence and foster a spirit of cooperation.

Staycations as alternatives can provide the same thrills as vacations without the high costs. Local adventures can be just as enriching and fun. Plan visits to nearby attractions like museums, parks, or community events. You might discover hidden gems in your own town that offer educational and entertaining experiences. A staycation can include activities such as hiking local trails, having a picnic at a scenic spot, or even transforming your home into a themed getaway. For instance, you could have a Hawaiian luau in your backyard, complete with decorations, music, and food. By engaging in these economical and accessible adventures, families can enjoy quality time together while also appreciating the community they live in.

Documenting Travel Memories is a wonderful way to preserve the magic of these adventures and strengthen emotional connections. Encourage each family member to keep a travel journal where they can write about their experiences, feelings, and favorite moments. This practice allows everyone to reflect on the journeys and appreciate the time spent together. Additionally, assembling photo albums or scrapbooks can be a creative family project that extends the enjoyment of trips long after they've ended. Looking back at these memories can reignite the joy of the experiences and serve as a reminder of the strong bonds formed through these shared adventures.

Involving everyone in the creation of these traditions is key. When children have a say in what activities to pursue, they feel more invested and excited about participating. This involvement not only empowers them but also fosters a sense of belonging and collaboration within the family. It transforms family members from passive participants to active co-creators of their own happiness and togetherness.

An important aspect of these traditions is their ability to be flexible and adaptable. Life after divorce can be unpredictable, and maintaining rigid schedules may not always be feasible. By approaching these adventures with flexibility, you allow room for spontaneity and creativity. For example, if an annual camping trip isn't possible one year, consider a weekend barbecue and tent setup in the backyard instead. The key is to focus on the quality of time spent together rather than the specific activity.

Moreover, these family adventures can contribute to personal growth and development. As children navigate new environments and situations, they learn valuable life skills such as problem-solving, teamwork, and resilience. Parents too can benefit from stepping out of their comfort zones and embracing new experiences alongside their children. These adventures create a supportive environment where everyone can grow individually and collectively.

To further enhance the bonding experience, consider integrating mini traditions within these larger ones. For instance, during the annual camping trip, you might have a nightly ritual of sharing stories around the campfire or a special song that everyone sings before bed. These small, consistent elements can add an extra layer of connection and anticipation to the main tradition.

Another idea is to mix and match different types of adventures to keep things interesting. One year, you might go on a big road trip, while the next year focuses on a series of smaller local adventures. This variety keeps the tradition fresh and exciting, ensuring that everyone looks forward to it each year.

As you embark on this journey of creating new family traditions, remember that the ultimate goal is to cultivate a stronger, more cohesive family unit. The adventures you choose should reflect your family's unique dynamics and preferences. Whether it's through a meticulously planned vacation or an impromptu staycation, the essence lies in spending time together, creating memories, and building a foundation of love and support.

Incorporating Cultural and Familial Practices
Celebrating Heritage and Integrating Cultural Elements into New Traditions

When it comes to creating new, meaningful traditions after a divorce, one powerful way to strengthen family bonds is by celebrating your heritage and integrating cultural elements. This approach not only honors the past but also helps establish a sense of identity and belonging in your children. Here are some creative ways to do just that.

Cultural Education Nights

Establishing Cultural Education Nights can be both fun and educational. Dedicating one evening each week to explore different cultures can foster empathy and broader perspectives in your children. Imagine transforming your living room into an Italian bistro one night and then a Japanese tea house the next. These evenings can include watching cultural documentaries, cooking traditional dishes, and even learning a few phrases in another language. For instance, you could make sushi together while watching a documentary on Japanese culture. This not only makes for a fun activity but also teaches respect and appreciation for different ways of life.

Kids often enjoy hands-on activities. Hence, incorporating arts and crafts into these nights can be particularly engaging. Making Greek pottery replicas or Native American dreamcatchers can turn into a memorable family project. While you're at it, discuss the significance behind these artifacts and what they represent in their respective cultures. These discussions can spur curiosity and encourage children to think critically about the world around them.

To keep things interesting, rotate the responsibility of choosing a culture to explore among family members. This practice ensures everyone feels included and excited about participating. A small guideline here: make sure to set aside time before the actual event to gather materials and plan activities—this preparation will make the night smoother and more enjoyable for everyone.

Participation in Community Events
Another effective method to connect your family with cultural heritages is through participation in community events. Local cultural festivals and celebrations provide an excellent opportunity to reconnect with the community and learn customs directly. Think of how much richer your weekends could be if you attended

a Chinese New Year parade or celebrated Diwali with local families. These experiences can instill a sense of pride and broaden your children's horizons.

Many communities offer cultural fairs, food festivals, and music events that showcase various traditions. Joining these events can be an eye-opening experience for kids. They get to see firsthand how other people celebrate their heritage, thereby fostering a deeper understanding and acceptance of diversity. Participating in such events can also serve as a bridge to forming new friendships and support networks among families going through similar transitions.

For a more immersive experience, consider volunteering at these events. Volunteering offers a dual benefit: it teaches your children the value of giving back to the community while allowing them to engage actively in the celebration. This involvement can be deeply rewarding and can help instill a lifelong love and respect for cultural heritage.

Learning Family Heritage
Encouraging your kids to research ancestry and explore family history can spark meaningful discussions and instill a sense of pride in their identity. Create activities that make this exploration interactive and exciting. For example, use genealogy websites to construct a family tree together. Gather photos, letters, and mementos from older family members and create a family history scrapbook.

One engaging way to dive into family heritage is through storytelling. Pass down tales from previous generations that reflect your family's journey and values. As you recount these stories, emphasize the resilience, courage, and perseverance that characterize your family's past. Such narratives not only bring the family closer but also help children understand where they come from and who they are.

Photos and memorabilia hold immense storytelling power. Dedicate a day to sitting down with your kids and go through old photo albums or home videos. Discuss the people and events captured in those moments. Explain what life was like for their ancestors, what traditions have been passed down, and why they are important. By linking the past with the present, you create a continuous thread of family history that your children can cherish and pass on.

Celebrating Cultural Holidays

Honoring important cultural holidays is another meaningful way to integrate heritage into your new family traditions. Celebrating holidays like Hanukkah, Kwanzaa, or Ramadan can increase awareness and appreciation of one's cultural identity. These occasions offer rich opportunities to teach your children about their roots while having fun together.

Preparation is crucial when it comes to celebrating cultural holidays. Plan ahead to gather necessary items, whether it's special decorations, traditional foods, or specific religious artifacts. Use this planning phase to educate your children about the holiday's history and significance. For instance, while preparing for Día De Muertos, explain the tradition of creating altars to honor deceased loved ones and what each item placed on the altar represents.

Food plays a significant role in these celebrations. Cooking traditional meals provides a tasty avenue to teaching heritage. Invite your children into the kitchen and assign them tasks appropriate to their age. Explain the recipes and ingredients, sharing stories about how these dishes have been passed down through generations. Packing traditional meals for school lunches can even turn into a conversation starter, helping your child share their culture with peers.

In addition to food, music, dance, and crafts can round out the celebration. Teach your kids traditional songs or dances related to the holiday. Create crafts that symbolize the festival; for example, making lanterns for the Mid-Autumn Festival or decorating eggs for Orthodox Easter. These activities enrich the celebration and create lasting memories.

Closing Remarks

As we wrap up our dive into creating new family traditions, it's clear that these little rituals can bring a lot of joy and unity to your post-divorce family life. From cooking up a storm with unique holiday recipes to engaging in outdoor adventures, every activity has the potential to create cherished memories and build stronger connections. Your kids can pitch in their ideas, ensuring everyone feels valued and heard. These moments not only offer an escape from daily stresses but also foster collaboration and trust among family members.

Embracing flexibility and humor is key to making these traditions stick. Whether you're setting up an annual photo booth or holding a Family Tradition Meeting, keep it light-hearted and fun. The goal is to weave a fabric of connection, laughter, and shared stories that your family will treasure for years to come. By establishing these new rituals, you're laying down a foundation of love, support, and togetherness, helping your children grow into well-rounded individuals who cherish their family bonds.

NINE
Educational Success: Supporting School and Academics

Educational success starts at home, and setting up a supportive learning environment can make all the difference for your child. Imagine turning your living room into an inspiring classroom where creativity meets discipline. You don't need to spend a fortune or remodel your house; a few simple tweaks can transform everyday spaces into havens of productivity. Picture this: a world where clutter vanishes, study zones appear like magic, and educational tools are as exciting as treasure hunts. It's all about creating a balance that invites curiosity and fosters focus, making homework not just a chore but a time of discovery.

In this chapter, we'll explore practical strategies to enhance your child's academic journey—starting with cobweb-free corners by decluttering the learning space and setting up organized, distraction-free zones. We'll delve into the treasure trove of educational resources beyond just textbooks, like interactive apps and online courses, that can fuel a love for learning. Moreover, we'll discuss how a consistent homework routine can banish last-minute panic attacks and bring a sense of calm. There's also room for fun, with enriching activities like arts and crafts to boost creativity and problem-solving skills. And let's not forget about building emotional resilience through strong parent-child bonds.

So, buckle up! We're about to turn your home into the ultimate launchpad for educational success.

Building a Scholastic-Friendly Home Environment

Creating a supportive home environment is crucial for your child's educational success. You might be surprised at how simple changes can make a big difference. Let's dive into some friendly and straightforward strategies to enhance your child's learning experience.

First things first: decluttering and organizing the learning space. A tidy workspace does wonders for focus and productivity. Imagine trying to concentrate in a room filled with distractions like scattered toys, piles of papers, and buzzing electronics. It's almost impossible! When you clear out the clutter, you create an environment where your child can zone in on their studies without unnecessary interruptions. Start by designating a specific area for homework and study time—ideally somewhere quiet and free from distractions like televisions or noisy siblings. Equip this space with all the necessary supplies such as pens, pencils, notebooks, and a comfortable chair. This designated learning zone signals to your child that it's time to get serious about their schoolwork when they sit down.

Now, let's talk about incorporating educational tools and resources. The more access your child has to diverse learning materials, the more they'll develop a love for learning and curiosity about the world around them. Think beyond textbooks and consider fun, interactive resources like educational apps, science kits, and online courses. There's a wealth of materials out there that can make learning exciting and engaging. For example, having an assortment of books on various topics available encourages your child to read about subjects that interest them. Libraries, both physical and digital, are treasure troves of knowledge waiting to be explored. You don't have to break the bank either; many local libraries offer free access to e-books and educational software. Show your child how to use these tools effectively, and you'll likely see their enthusiasm for learning skyrocket.

Another key aspect is setting specific times for homework. Establishing a routine helps children develop effective study habits and manage their time better. Just like adults benefit from a regular work schedule, kids thrive on consistency. Having a set time each day dedicated solely to homework ensures that it becomes a part of their daily routine rather than a sporadic activity. Whether it's right after school, following dinner, or before bedtime, choose a slot that works best for your family's schedule and stick to it. This consistency helps reduce procrastination and last-minute cramming, making for a much smoother academic journey. Encourage your child to take short breaks during longer study sessions to keep their mind fresh and focused. Breaks involving physical activity can be especially beneficial, as they help release pent-up energy and improve concentration.

But academics aren't just about hitting the books. Encouraging creativity and exploration through enrichment activities like arts and crafts plays a crucial role in balanced development. These activities provide a much-needed break from structured learning, offering an outlet for self-expression and critical thinking. When your child engages in painting, sculpting, or crafting, they're not only building fine motor skills but also learning to think outside the box. These creative pursuits foster problem-solving abilities and innovation, skills that are highly valuable in academic settings and beyond. Set aside time each week for these enriching activities. Provide different materials and ideas, but let your child lead the way. Their creations may surprise you!

Additionally, fostering a nurturing atmosphere is essential. A strong emotional foundation allows children to navigate educational challenges with greater resilience. Secure parent-child relationships lead to higher engagement, motivation, and achievement in school. By creating a home environment where children feel valued and encouraged, parents can alleviate stress and anxiety, enabling their children to approach academic pursuits confidently.

Let's say you've organized the workspace, stocked up on educational tools, set a homework routine, and planned some art projects. What's next? Never underestimate the power of quality time. Amidst busy schedules, carving out moments to connect with your child makes a significant difference. Simple activities like shared meals, discussing their day, or playing games together strengthen your bond and build a sense of security. This connection is vital; when children feel supported and understood at home, they're more likely to transfer that confidence and stability to their academic endeavors.

Sometimes, life throws curveballs. Financial constraints, work demands, or personal struggles can make it challenging to maintain an ideal learning environment. It's important to remember that creating a nurturing home doesn't require perfection. Prioritizing even small gestures of support can have a lasting impact. Adapting to individual needs is crucial. Every child learns differently, and recognizing these differences can help tailor your approach to meet their unique requirements. Explore alternative learning methods and seek support from educators when needed.

Let's not forget the community surrounding us. Building a support network can be invaluable. Community resources like after-school programs, tutoring services, or counseling can provide additional academic support. Connecting with other parents facing similar challenges can offer advice and a sense of shared experience.

In this digital age, technology can be a double-edged sword. Used wisely, it can be a powerful tool for learning. Educational apps, online resources, and virtual tutoring platforms can supplement traditional methods. However, parental guidance is crucial to ensure that technology remains productive and complements the nurturing home environment.

Balancing structure with relaxation is another tip. While routines are essential, so is downtime. Children need moments to unwind and pursue extracurricular interests. This balance supports academic achievement and overall well-being.

Encouraging Regular Study Habits

There's a specific kind of magic that happens when kids develop effective study habits: they start managing their time better, understanding their responsibilities, and overall, excel in their academics. But how do we sprinkle that magical dust on them? Let's delve into some practical strategies to help kids get organized and study effectively, all while keeping things light-hearted and fun.

First off, let's talk about introducing tools like planners. Imagine giving your child a trusty planner, much like a sidekick in a superhero movie. This tool can be indispensable for tracking assignments and deadlines. A planner helps children visualize their tasks ahead and reduces the overwhelming feeling that often accompanies schoolwork. It's like handing them a map to navigate through the dense jungle of homework and projects. Encourage them to mark due dates, break down big assignments into smaller tasks, and check off completed work. Over time, this habit will make them more aware of the ticking clock. It's about making sure those "oops, I forgot" moments turn into "got it all covered" triumphs.

Creating a study schedule is another crucial step. Much like setting up camp in our jungle analogy, having a schedule instills discipline and minimizes the dreaded last-minute cramming sessions. When children know they have set times dedicated to studying, they're less likely to scramble at the eleventh hour. For example, Joan Greenfield, a second-grade teacher from West Hartford, CT, emphasizes the importance of holding grade-schoolers accountable for their assignments and understanding the natural consequences of not completing them. She implements something called Choice Time every Friday where students get to enjoy leisure activities only if they've finished all their assignments. This teaches kids that good things— like free time and reduced stress—follow when they manage their time wisely.

Now, let's introduce self-assessment into the mix. Think of it as your child's inner compass, helping them navigate their educational journey with critical thinking and awareness of their learning styles. Self-assessment encourages kids to reflect on what they've learned and identify areas they might need to revisit. It's essential for developing metacognitive skills, or simply put, thinking about thinking. By regularly asking questions like "What did I find easy?" and "Which parts were challenging?", children begin to understand their strengths and weaknesses. This reflection can then guide their future study sessions, making them more efficient learners.

However, let's not forget the importance of staying engaged with your child's academic life through discussions and support. Imagine you're a seasoned explorer guiding your young adventurer through unfamiliar terrain. Regular conversations about what they're learning, the challenges they're facing, and their successes are invaluable. These discussions show your child that you're invested in their education, offering both emotional support and practical help. For instance, set aside some time each evening to discuss their day and what they've accomplished. Celebrate their victories, no matter how small, and provide encouragement when they hit a rough patch. This involvement fosters a sense of security and motivation, making them feel less alone on their journey.

Establishing priorities is another important step. Children often have to juggle several tasks simultaneously, from schoolwork to extracurricular activities to playtime. Teaching them how to differentiate between 'have tos' and 'want tos' is essential. Some educators suggest using a visual aid like the rock, pebble, and water analogy to help kids prioritize their tasks. Rocks symbolize the most important duties (school, homework, sleep), pebbles represent secondary obligations (extracurricular activities), and water stands for leisure activities (video games, hanging out with friends).

When tackling long-term assignments, breaking down the project into manageable chunks can be a lifesaver. Picture the assignment as a giant boulder that needs to be chipped away gradually. Amy Broocke suggests dividing a task into smaller steps, such as reading chapters over a few nights or gathering materials well ahead of time. Sticky notes can be helpful here; they allow flexibility if tasks take longer than expected. Planning backward from the due date ensures that your child knows exactly what needs to be done and by when, making the assignment seem far less daunting.

Finally, a word about parental involvement. Encouraging your child to engage in regular dialogue with their teachers can be incredibly beneficial. Let them take responsibility for explaining missed assignments or seeking clarification on complex topics. The goal is to reduce hovering and nagging, thereby fostering independence and self-advocacy in your child. Helping your child build a supportive relationship with their educators also opens avenues for additional academic assistance and resources.

Collaborating with Teachers and School Staff

Building relationships with educators is paramount in supporting your child's learning journey. One of the first steps you can take is to maintain regular communication with teachers. By staying in touch, you become more aware of your child's academic progress and behavior in school. This constant flow of information helps you address any challenges early on and recognize your child's achievements. Instead of waiting for report cards, consider reaching out periodically through emails, phone calls, or scheduled meetings. Frequent check-ins ensure that you're not only updated on your child's performance but also actively involved in their educational experience.

Attending parent-teacher conferences is another crucial aspect. These conferences provide a structured opportunity to discuss your child's strengths and areas for improvement directly with their teachers. Demonstrating your commitment by making these meetings a priority shows your child and their teachers that you value education. Conferences are not just about hearing from teachers; they're also an excellent time for you to ask questions and get insights on how to support your child better at home. Additionally, bringing up any concerns you have during these discussions can lead to collaborative problem-solving.

Being visible and participative in school functions and committees can significantly enhance your involvement. Participating in school activities such as open houses, sports events, or arts performances not only boosts your child's morale but also strengthens your connection with the school community. Volunteering for school committees or parent organizations can provide a platform for you to contribute to decision-making processes and advocate for important issues. Your active presence demonstrates to your child that their education matters to you, fostering a positive attitude toward learning and school engagement.

Another key way to support your child's education is by familiarizing yourself with available school resources like tutoring programs or counseling services. Schools often offer a range of support services aimed at helping students succeed academically and emotionally. Knowing what resources are available allows you to guide your child effectively when they need extra help. For instance, if your child struggles with a particular subject, enrolling them in a tutoring program can provide the additional support they need to improve. Similarly, if they face social or emotional challenges, counseling services can offer necessary guidance and support.

By staying in touch with teachers regularly, you create a partnership centered around your child's success. This ongoing dialogue ensures that both you and the teacher are on the same page regarding your child's development. It creates a supportive network where both parties can share observations and strategies that benefit the child. Regular updates can be achieved through various modes of communication such as messages, newsletters, or even quick chats during school drop-offs and pick-ups. The goal is to keep the lines of communication open and consistent.

Making attendance at parent-teacher conferences non-negotiable helps you get a comprehensive view of your child's academic life. These meetings are invaluable in understanding the nuances of your child's performance and behavior in class. Teachers can highlight specific areas that need attention and suggest practical ways to address them. It's also an opportune moment for you to share insights about your child's learning habits and preferences at home. Such reciprocal communication fosters a deeper understanding and alignment in supporting the child's educational needs.

Active participation in school functions has a twofold benefit: it keeps you engaged in your child's school life and shows your child that you are there for them. When children see their parents involved, they tend to take their own responsibilities more seriously. Your involvement can make school environments feel more inclusive and supportive. Whether it's attending a school play or joining a fundraising committee, your contributions add value and show your child that their school endeavors are important to you.

Understanding and utilizing school resources can significantly benefit your child's academic journey. Many schools offer specialized programs to cater to diverse student needs, from gifted programs to special education services. By becoming acquainted with these resources, you position yourself to better support your child in navigating any academic hurdles they may encounter. Engaging with counselors or specialists can also equip you with strategies to reinforce learning at home, ensuring a holistic approach to your child's education.

Addressing Academic Challenges Quickly
It's 7:30 a.m. and you can already hear the sound of grumbling from your child's room about yet another test they forgot to study for. As a parent, it's crucial to be Sherlock Holmes when it comes to recognizing signs of academic struggles. Declining grades? Check.

Avoidance of schoolwork? Double check. Maybe your child has even become the master of the mysterious "vanishing homework" trick. These are all clues that something is amiss in their academic world.

Now, here's where we get proactive. Once you've put on your detective hat and recognized these signs, it's time to collaborate with both your child and their teachers to develop a support plan. Picture this like assembling a superhero team. The mission? To tackle these academic challenges head-on. Call a meeting with the teacher, discuss the issues openly, and collectively come up with action steps. Whether it's extra tutoring, changing study methods, or even adjusting classroom seating arrangements, every bit helps. Just remember, you're not forming this plan alone; involve your child in the discussion too. They are, after all, the star of this superhero saga.

Next, let's talk about creating an open environment at home where your children can freely discuss their academic woes without fearing they'll be judged. It's easier said than done, right? Think of it as running a non-judgmental talk show, where your child is the guest star allowed to vent, express concerns, and share their thoughts. You can start by asking open-ended questions like, "What part of your school day do you find most challenging?" or "How do you feel about your upcoming tests?" Such questions encourage them to open up, shedding light on what might be going wrong. Your job? Listen carefully and keep the judgment monster locked away in the basement.

Of course, Rome wasn't built in a day, and neither will your child's newfound academic success emerge overnight. Regular evaluation of the support plan's effectiveness is essential. Think of it like tracking the progress of a fitness regime—monitoring milestones, tweaking exercises, and celebrating those hard-earned six-pack abs (metaphorically speaking, of course). Set regular check-ins with both the teacher and your child. Ask questions like, "Is the new study method helping?" or "Do you think the extra tutoring is making a difference?"

But let's not forget to celebrate the small victories along the way. Did they go from a D to a C on that math test? Bust out a mini celebration! Positive reinforcement can be incredibly motivating. Maybe it's as simple as letting them pick the movie for family night or a little more screen time on the weekend. Small rewards can provide the encouragement they need to keep pushing forward.

And let's sprinkle some humor here. Imagine turning study time into a game show called "Who Wants to Be a Math Champion?" With you as the quirky host throwing in funny comments, and your child as the eager contestant. By transforming mundane study sessions into enjoyable experiences, you're also breaking down the fear associated with difficult subjects.

Sometimes, however, despite all efforts, professional intervention might be needed. Whether it's specialized tutoring, counseling, or even an educational psychologist, don't hesitate to seek help if you find yourself hitting a dead end. It's like calling in reinforcements when you're stuck in a particularly tricky level of a video game.

Let's recap, shall we? Recognizing academic struggles early on is your first clue. Collaboratively setting up an action plan makes you the team leader. Fostering an open discussion environment turns you into the loving talk show host. Regularly evaluating the plan ensures you stay on track, much like a diligent fitness coach. Celebrating milestones makes you the joyous cheerleader who keeps spirits high. And when things get tough, seeking professional help makes you the wise parent who knows when to call in the pros.

Final Thoughts

Looking back at everything we've talked about, it's clear that creating a supportive home environment is like being the ultimate cheerleader for your child's education. From decluttering their study space to setting up a solid homework routine, these steps help them focus and build good study habits. And let's not forget the fun stuff – books, educational apps, and even creative projects can turn learning into an exciting adventure! By taking these actions, you're setting the stage for your child to thrive academically and develop a lifelong love for learning.

But life isn't always a smooth ride, and sometimes challenges pop up. It's important to recognize when things aren't going well and to jump into action with support plans, open communication, and plenty of encouragement. Collaborating with teachers and using community resources can make a huge difference too. Remember, it's not about being perfect; it's about making those small, meaningful gestures that show your child they're supported and understood. With a little humor, a lot of heart, and some strategic moves, you'll be helping your child navigate through the ups and downs of their educational journey.

TEN

Financial Planning
for Single Dads

Securing financial stability as a single dad might seem like trying to solve the countries financial deficite, but worry not, we're here to make the path smoother and a touch more entertaining. With a practical approach and a sprinkle of humor, you'll find your footing in no time. Post-divorce budgeting can feel like navigating through an unfamiliar jungle, filled with new expenses and unexpected financial turns. But hey, if Indiana Jones could survive snakes and booby traps, you can certainly conquer a few spreadsheets and receipts!

In this chapter, we dive deep into the essentials of managing your finances effectively as a single father. You'll start by assessing your new financial landscape—think of it as taking an inventory before embarking on a grand adventure. Next, we'll walk you through crafting a realistic budget that keeps ramen noodles as an occasional treat rather than your primary food group. To help you stay on track, we'll explore different budgeting methods tailored to fit your unique needs, from zero-based budgeting to the 50/30/20 rule. You'll also discover the magic of budgeting apps, which can turn tracking expenses into a task as simple as ordering pizza online. And because life loves to throw curveballs, building an emergency fund will be emphasized as your financial safety net. We'll even sneak in some tips on lifestyle adjustments that don't require sacrificing all the fun. Sprinkle in ideas for generating extra income and professional guidance when needed, and you'll have a comprehensive guide to financial planning. Ready to transform those financial woes into financial wows? Let's get started!

Budgeting Effectively Post-Divorce

Creating and maintaining a budget post-divorce can feel like navigating uncharted waters. However, with some practical steps and a dash of patience, you can sail through it smoothly. Let's dive in and tackle the process head-on.

First and foremost, assessing your new financial landscape is crucial. Post-divorce, your income and expenses will likely look quite different. Maybe you're no longer splitting household costs or perhaps you've taken on additional responsibilities. Start by listing all sources of income, including child support or alimony if applicable. Next, itemize your regular expenses. These might include housing, utilities, groceries, transportation, and any new solo expenditures. Don't forget to account for infrequent but significant expenses like annual insurance premiums or vehicle maintenance.

Once you've identified your new financial situation, it's time to create a realistic budget. Honesty is key here. Pretending you can survive on a shoestring budget won't help anyone. Aim for accuracy, not austerity. If you spend $200 a month on groceries, don't try to shave it down unrealistically to $50; after all, living off ramen noodles isn't the healthiest (or most delicious) long-term plan.

Now that you've got a grip on your current financial picture, let's talk about developing a budgeting method tailored to your needs. Among the many budgeting frameworks, two popular ones are zero-based budgeting and the 50/30/20 rule. Zero-based budgeting means assigning every dollar a job until you reach zero. This method ensures you consciously allocate funds to savings, necessities, and discretionary spending.

On the other hand, the 50/30/20 rule simplifies things: allocate 50% of your income to necessities, 30% to wants, and 20% to savings or debt repayment. This method offers flexibility and keeps you from feeling restricted. Whichever method you choose, consistency is vital. Stick to it, adjust when necessary, and don't be too hard on yourself if you occasionally falter. We all have those months where the car breaks down exactly when gym fees and kids' school supplies are due.

In today's digital age, there are numerous tools and resources at your disposal to make this process even smoother. Budgeting apps like Mint, YNAB (You Need A Budget), or PocketGuard can help track expenses, set savings goals, and alert you when you're veering off course. The beauty of these apps is their ability to sync with your accounts, providing real-time updates and saving you the hassle of manual entry.

While budgeting apps are fantastic, setting aside an emergency fund is non-negotiable. Life's unpredictable and having a safety net can mean the difference between a minor inconvenience and a financial crisis. Aim to save enough to cover three to six months' worth of living expenses. Start small if you need to; even stashing away a few bucks a week can add up over time. Consider funneling any extra money—like tax refunds, bonuses, or that $20 bill you found in the old jacket—into your emergency fund.

As you're building this safety net, reflect on where you can tweak your lifestyle without sacrificing too much joy. For instance, can you opt for a smaller apartment or switch to public transportation? Cutting cable in favor of streaming services can also free up some cash. Remember, living below your means doesn't equate to living miserably. It's about making conscious choices to build a more secure future.

Generating extra income can also be a game-changer. From selling unused items online to picking up a side gig like freelance writing, there's no shortage of ways to boost your earnings. Just ensure these endeavors don't eat into your essential parenting time. Balancing your role as a father and financial provider takes finesse but finding that sweet spot is entirely possible.

Lastly, don't hesitate to seek professional guidance if needed. Financial planners or advisors can provide personalized assistance tailored to your specific situation. Sometimes an outside perspective is just what you need to see clearly through the fog of numbers and obligations.

Saving for Your Children's Future

Saving for your children's education and future expenses is one of the smartest financial moves a single dad can make. Not only does this ensure financial stability, but it also sets a strong foundation for your children's future. Let's dive into some relevant options, discuss their benefits, and offer practical advice on how to instill good saving habits in your kids.

Firstly, let's discuss college savings accounts. One popular option is the 529 plan, which offers tax advantages that are tough to beat. Contributions grow deferred from federal and state income taxes, and qualified withdrawals—those used for tuition, certain room and board fees, supplies, and books—are tax-free. This means more of your hard-earned money goes directly toward your child's education rather than getting eaten up by taxes. Many states also provide additional state tax advantages, making it even more beneficial for in-state residents.

Beyond these tax benefits, the 529 plan offers flexibility and control. You decide how the funds are spent, whether it's paying the college directly or reimbursing yourself for qualified expenses. And should circumstances change, like if your child earns a scholarship or joins the military, you can withdraw funds without penalties (but taxes may still apply). Essentially, the 529 plan provides a safety net, ensuring your investment is protected while still flexible enough to adapt to life's unexpected turns.

Next, let's introduce the concept of involving children in their future savings, which is a fantastic way to teach financial literacy. Including your kids in discussions about their education-saving goals can have long-lasting impacts. For example, let them see how much is being saved each month and explain how compound interest works. When children understand the effort and planning behind their education fund, they're likely to value their education more and be more responsible with money in general.

Now, about structuring lessons around everyday activities—this doesn't have to be complicated! Small, consistent actions can build a solid foundation in financial understanding. Take grocery shopping as an example. Give your child a small budget and let them help decide what to buy for the week. This teaches them about budgeting and making choices based on priorities. Similarly, you could involve them in saving for a family outing. Set a goal and track progress together, showing them how saving bit by bit can lead to rewarding results.

Another fun, educational activity is setting up a 'family bank,' where your children can deposit portions of their allowance or birthday money. Offer a small interest rate to mimic real savings accounts. This not only makes saving exciting but also gives them a tangible sense of how money can grow over time.

Lastly, many parents overlook grants and scholarships when planning for education expenses, yet these resources can significantly reduce the financial burden. Begin exploring these options early. Websites like Fastweb and College Board offer databases packed with scholarship opportunities categorized by various criteria—like academic achievements, community service, and even creative pursuits. Encourage your kids to actively seek out and apply for these scholarships. It's never too early to start building a portfolio of accomplishments and essays that can be used to apply for multiple scholarships.

Additionally, federal grants like the Pell Grant provide substantial aid to students from low-income families. Make sure to fill out the Free Application for Federal Student Aid (FAFSA) as early as possible to determine eligibility. Keep an eye out for state-specific grants and institutional scholarships offered by colleges themselves, as these can also add up to significant savings.

To sum up, here are some immediate steps:

Set Up a 529 Plan: Look into the various options available in your state and start contributing regularly. The earlier you start, the more time your money has to grow.

Involve Your Kids: Make saving and budgeting a family affair. Share the goals and show them the progress. This fosters a sense of responsibility and financial literacy.

Everyday Learning: Incorporate small teaching moments into daily life. Use activities like grocery shopping and saving for outings to impart valuable lessons.

Explore Grants and Scholarships: Research and apply for every applicable grant and scholarship. The more proactive you are, the less financial strain you'll face.

Investing in Insurance Policies

Insurance is a cornerstone of financial planning, especially for single dads looking to secure their families' future. Let's dive into essential insurance considerations that can provide peace of mind and financial stability.

First on our list is life insurance. Imagine this: you're the rock for your children, providing not just love and guidance but also financial support. Now, think about what would happen if you were suddenly not there. Life insurance steps in to fill that void, ensuring your kids are financially protected even after you're gone. A good life insurance policy provides a death benefit to your beneficiaries, which can cover everyday expenses, education costs, or even help them buy a home one day. In simple terms, it's like leaving an umbrella to your kids for rainy days when you can't be around. If this isn't included in your financial plan, it's high time to reconsider. Trust me, securing financial stability for your little ones is one of the best legacies you can leave behind.

Next up, navigating health coverage might seem daunting, but it's crucial. Health insurance protects you from staggering medical bills and ensures you and your children get the healthcare you need without breaking the bank. Start with employer-provided plans, if available. They often offer robust coverage at reasonable rates. If that's not an option, explore government programs like Medicaid or the Children's Health Insurance Program (CHIP) for your kids. Private health insurance is another route, though it tends to be pricier. Either way, make sure the plan covers essential benefits such as doctor visits, hospital stays, prescriptions, and preventive care. Also, look into Health Savings Accounts (HSAs) or Flexible Spending Accounts (FSAs). These accounts let you set aside pre-tax dollars to pay for eligible medical expenses, offering a nifty way to save while staying healthy.

Now let's talk about disability insurance. This often-overlooked policy is a lifesaver if you ever find yourself unable to work due to illness or injury. Picture this: you're suddenly unable to earn your paycheck, yet the bills keep piling up. Disability insurance provides a portion of your income during these tough times, making sure you can still cover everyday expenses like rent, groceries, and utilities. There are two primary types: short-term and long-term disability insurance. Short-term policies kick in quicker but typically last only a few months to a year. Long-term policies have a longer waiting period but can cover you for several years or even until retirement. Opting for both gives you a safety net regardless of the situation's duration. Working with an insurance agent can help tailor a plan that meets your needs and fits your budget.

Finally, let's discuss umbrella insurance. Think of it as an extra layer of protection that kicks in when your other policies max out. It's particularly useful for defending against large claims that could otherwise bankrupt you. Suppose you're held liable for an accident and the damages exceed your auto insurance limit. Your umbrella policy picks up where auto insurance leaves off, covering the remaining costs. This type of insurance can also protect you against lawsuits over property damage, injuries, and even slander or defamation. It's relatively affordable compared to the extensive coverage it offers. For example, a $1 million policy might cost just a few hundred dollars a year. Given its wide-ranging protection, umbrella insurance is a smart addition to any comprehensive financial plan.

Understanding and Managing Debt

Navigating the world of finances as a single dad can feel like being dropped in the middle of a maze with no map, especially when debt is part of the equation. Tackling debt head-on requires a solid game plan and a positive mindset. So, whether it feels like you're staring down an insurmountable mountain of bills or just trying to get ahead of your finances, here are some steps to help you conquer existing debt and pave the way for financial stability.

First things first, take a deep dive into your outstanding debt obligations. Grab a pen, paper, and maybe a strong cup of coffee because it's time to face those numbers! Begin by pulling up your latest credit report to get a comprehensive view of all your debts—this includes credit cards, loans, mortgages, and any other financial liabilities. List them out in detail: the creditor's name, total amount owed, interest rates, minimum monthly payments, and due dates.

With this list in front of you, prioritize which debts need immediate attention. Typically, it's wise to focus on high-interest debts first, as they tend to spiral out of control quickly if left unchecked. However, there are structured repayment methods that might suit your situation better: the avalanche method and the snowball method.

The avalanche method involves paying off debts with the highest interest rates first while making minimum payments on the rest. This method saves you money in the long run by reducing the amount paid in interest. On the flip side, the snowball method focuses on paying off the smallest debts first, regardless of the interest rate, to gain quick wins and build momentum. Both strategies have their merits, so choose the one that fits best with your financial personality and stick to it!

Next, consider negotiating with creditors. It may seem daunting, but creditors are often more willing to work with you than you might think. They prefer receiving some payment rather than none at all. Reach out to them directly and explain your current financial situation. Ask if they can lower the interest rate, extend the repayment period, or even settle for a lower amount. Negotiation can result in more manageable payments and prevent your debts from ballooning further. Remember, clear communication and honesty about your circumstances can go a long way in finding a mutually agreeable solution.

Life as a single dad is unpredictable, and financial difficulties can strike at any moment. Hence, it's crucial to implement lifestyle changes to minimize the likelihood of accumulating more debt. Start by creating a realistic budget that cuts unnecessary expenses and focuses on essentials. Dining out? Consider meal prepping instead. Expensive gym membership? Try home workouts or local parks. Review every purchase and ask yourself, "Is this necessary?"

One of the most effective ways to shield yourself from future debt is by establishing an emergency fund. Yes, having an emergency fund might sound like a luxury when managing existing debts, but it's a crucial safety net. Set aside a small amount of money each month, even if it's just $20. Over time, these contributions will accumulate into a buffer for unexpected expenses—whether it's an urgent car repair or a medical bill. Having an emergency fund ensures you're not forced to rely on credit cards or loans when emergencies arise, keeping you from sinking deeper into debt.

Additionally, involving your children in the conversation about finances can foster a sense of responsibility and awareness. Explain to them, in age-appropriate terms, why certain sacrifices are necessary and how everyone's efforts contribute to the family's financial health. This not only helps them understand the value of money but also builds a supportive environment where they feel included.

To make these financial strategies stick, consider seeking professional advice. Financial advisors or credit counselors can offer personalized guidance tailored to your unique situation. They provide insights on debt management, budgeting techniques, and long-term financial planning, helping you navigate the complexities more effectively. Don't hesitate to reach out; sometimes an external perspective can illuminate solutions you hadn't considered.

Facing and managing debt is undoubtedly challenging, but with conscientious effort and a clear strategy, it's entirely possible to regain control over your finances. Evaluate your debts honestly, choose a repayment method that works for you, negotiate with creditors where you can, and adopt lifestyle changes that prevent future debt accumulation. By fostering open communication within your family and seeking professional help when needed, you'll build a secure financial foundation that benefits both you and your children.

Final Thoughts

Securing financial stability as a single father isn't just about crunching numbers; it's about making smart, practical choices that ensure a brighter future for you and your kids. In this chapter, we've explored how to budget effectively post-divorce, using tools like zero-based budgeting and the 50/30/20 rule to keep your finances in check without sacrificing all your comforts.

We've talked about the importance of having an emergency fund stashed away for those unexpected expenses that life loves to throw our way. By making small adjustments like choosing streaming services over traditional cable or picking up a side gig, you can boost your income and savings without feeling overwhelmed.

On top of budgeting, investing in insurance policies is crucial. Life, health, disability, and umbrella insurance provide layers of protection for you and your children, ensuring that even if things go awry, you'll have a safety net. And don't forget to save for your children's future through options like 529 college savings plans. By involving your kids in financial discussions and teaching them good money habits through everyday activities, you're setting them up for a financially savvy future. Remember, managing debt effectively involves honest assessments and strategic repayments—whether you choose the avalanche or snowball method. Seeking professional guidance when needed can help you tailor these strategies to your unique situation. Balancing your role as a financial provider and a nurturing father may seem like an impossible task, but with consistency and a touch of patience, you've got this!

ELEVEN
Becoming a Mentor and Role Model

Becoming a mentor and role model for your children is a journey filled with opportunities to grow both as a parent and as an individual. Picture this: you're not just any dad, but the superhero in sneakers who teaches life lessons while making breakfast or driving to soccer practice. Your mission, should you choose to accept it, involves guiding your kids toward becoming successful and confident adults. But how do you achieve such a heroic feat? By instilling essential values, encouraging independence, providing unwavering support, and promoting lifelong learning.

In this chapter, we'll embark on an adventure through the intricacies of mentoring your children. Get ready to dive deep into practical strategies for embedding core values into their daily lives, like honesty, integrity, empathy, and respect. We'll explore how to turn everyday moments into lessons that foster independence and problem-solving skills. You'll learn the fine art of balancing guidance with freedom, creating an environment where your kids feel empowered to make decisions and learn from their experiences. Along the way, we'll also discuss how to support their educational and career goals without turning into a helicopter parent. So, sit back as we set off on this enlightening journey to becoming the ultimate mentor and role model for your children.

Instilling Values and Ethics

Teaching children foundational values and ethics is akin to giving them a roadmap for life. These core values shape their character, guide their conduct, and influence their decisions in myriad situations. The importance of these values cannot be overstated; they are the bedrock upon which confident and responsible adults are built.

Understanding the importance of core values begins with recognizing your role in shaping a child's character and conduct. Core values like honesty, integrity, empathy, and respect serve as inner compasses that guide children through life's maze of choices. When children understand what these values mean and why they matter, they are more likely to incorporate them into their daily lives. For instance, a child who learns the value of honesty early on will likely grow up to be an adult who values transparency and truthfulness in relationships and work environments. This understanding helps children make decisions that are not only beneficial to themselves but also considerate of others.

Practical ways to teach values can make this abstract concept tangible for children. One effective strategy is storytelling. Whether through bedtime stories or real-life anecdotes, tales that emphasize moral lessons can leave a lasting impact. For example, sharing stories where characters face ethical dilemmas and make positive choices can help children see the values in action. Role-playing is another hands-on approach.

By acting out scenarios where ethical decisions need to be made, children get to practice and internalize these values. Involving children in community service projects or family volunteering activities can also be incredibly effective. These real-life experiences provide opportunities for children to witness the impact of compassion, responsibility, and teamwork, reinforcing their importance.

Encouraging a value-driven mindset has long-term benefits that extend well beyond childhood. When children adopt core values, they develop a framework for making decisions throughout their lives. This value-driven approach becomes particularly crucial during adolescence and adulthood, where peer pressure and societal influences intensify. By having a strong set of values to fall back on, children are better equipped to navigate these pressures confidently. Additionally, instilling a value-driven mindset fosters a sense of purpose and direction. Children who understand and appreciate core values are more likely to pursue goals and careers aligned with their principles, leading to more fulfilling and meaningful lives.

Setting a personal example is perhaps one of the most powerful ways to teach values to children. As the saying goes, actions speak louder than words. Fathers play a pivotal role in this regard. By embodying the values they wish to instill, dads can demonstrate the importance of these values in everyday life. For instance, when a father consistently shows kindness and respect to others, his children are likely to mirror this behavior.

Similarly, practicing honesty and taking responsibility for mistakes openly can teach children the importance of integrity and accountability. It's about living the values you want your children to embrace, creating a consistent and clear message about what truly matters.

One practical aspect of teaching values involves providing opportunities for ethical decision-making. Creating environments where children feel safe to explore and experiment with different values and perspectives allows them to practice making ethical decisions and learn from the consequences of their choices. This experiential learning is invaluable, as it not only reinforces the importance of ethical behavior but also helps children understand the complexities involved in making moral choices.

Empathy and compassion are fundamental values that deserve special emphasis. Encouraging children to consider the perspectives of others and to treat people with kindness and respect lays the groundwork for healthy and positive interactions. Practicing empathy can be as simple as discussing how others might feel in various situations or encouraging acts of kindness within the family and community. This focus on empathy helps children develop the social and emotional skills needed to forge meaningful relationships and contribute positively to society.

Challenges and considerations are inevitable in the journey of teaching moral values and ethics. Ensuring consistency and clarity of messaging among all adults in a child's life can be tricky. It's important for parents, caregivers, and educators to align on the values they wish to emphasize and present a unified front. Additionally, being mindful of each child's age and developmental stage is crucial, as strategies and approaches may need to be adjusted accordingly. Cultural and religious diversity also plays a significant role, requiring sensitivity and openness to different perspectives on moral behavior.

Balancing discipline and positive reinforcement is another delicate aspect. While appropriate discipline is necessary to reinforce positive behavior, it's equally important to provide children with opportunities to learn and grow from their mistakes. Encouraging discussion and reflection on decisions and their impacts can further support this learning process.

Addressing contemporary ethical issues is essential as society and technology continue to evolve. Staying informed about current challenges and guiding children on how to navigate these issues ethically equips them to handle modern-day dilemmas effectively. Teaching children to critically evaluate their assumptions, consider other viewpoints, and make thoughtful decisions prepares them for the complex world they will face as adults.

Encouraging Independence and Problem-Solving
Instilling a sense of independence in children is a vital component in their journey toward becoming confident, self-reliant adults. To help them navigate challenges and develop resilience, we need to create an

environment that encourages self-sufficiency and critical thinking.

Creating opportunities for independence can start with age-appropriate chores and tasks. Assigning such responsibilities helps children learn essential life skills while fostering a sense of accomplishment. For instance, toddlers can begin by putting away their toys or helping to make the bed with assistance. As they grow older, the complexity of their tasks can increase. A child ages 4-6 might set the table or sort laundry, while those aged 7-9 can make simple meals under supervision and fold laundry. By the time they reach 10 years and above, they can take on more complex tasks like cooking meals, doing laundry, or mowing the lawn. These activities not only teach responsibility but also build a child's confidence in their abilities.

Introducing problem-solving scenarios is another effective strategy. Engaging children in situations that require critical thinking promotes independence in a meaningful way. Suppose your child encounters a broken toy. Instead of immediately offering a solution, ask open-ended questions like, "What do you think we could do to fix this?" This allows them to brainstorm and explore potential solutions. Such experiences empower children to tackle problems head-on, equipping them with the tools needed to think creatively and analytically.

Encouraging resilience in the face of failure is equally important. Perseverance is a valuable skill that will serve children throughout their lives. When a child doesn't succeed at a task, it's crucial to highlight the effort they put in rather than solely focusing on the outcome. This approach helps them understand that setbacks are part of the learning process. For example, if a child struggles with a math problem, praising their attempts and guiding them through different problem-solving methods can nurture their determination. Consistency in expectations and regular reinforcement of positive behavior play a significant role in building resilience.

Modeling problem-solving behaviors sets a powerful example for children. Demonstrating how to face challenges effectively provides them with a blueprint to follow. Imagine you're faced with a tricky situation at work. Sharing your thought process with your child—how you identified the issue, considered various solutions, and ultimately resolved it—can be incredibly instructive. This transparency shows them that problem-solving involves patience, critical thinking, and resourcefulness. Additionally, involving them in everyday decision-making processes, like planning a family trip, helps them see these skills in action.

Incorporating practical skills and responsibilities into daily routines further reinforces independence. Breaking tasks into smaller, manageable steps can make even the most daunting chores approachable. For example, preparing for school can be divided into steps: choosing clothes, packing a school bag, and preparing lunch. Visual checklists can aid younger children in keeping track of these steps. This methodical approach teaches them organization and time-management skills.

Responsibility for personal readiness is another critical aspect. Teaching children to manage their time efficiently, especially in the morning, instills a sense of discipline. Tools like clocks and timers can help them gauge how much time they have for each task. Encouraging them to prepare for the next day in advance, such as setting out clothes or packing their school bag the night before, reduces morning stress and fosters planning skills. Self-care routines, including hygiene and grooming, reinforce the importance of taking responsibility for their well-being.

Empowering your child through goal setting is also beneficial. Setting small and achievable goals can help children recognize their strengths and areas for improvement. When they see progress towards a goal, it boosts their confidence and encourages continuous learning. For example, if a child sets a goal to read a certain number of books each month, tracking their progress and celebrating milestones can motivate them to keep pushing forward.

High expectations drive a child's achievement and independence. When parents convey a belief in their children's abilities, it motivates them to rise to the occasion. Encouraging effort over perfection helps children value hard work and persistence. Offering tasks slightly above their current skill levels challenges them to stretch their abilities and learn new things, reinforcing the notion that it's okay to struggle and that persistence is valuable.

Providing Career Guidance and Support

Helping your children identify interests and paths that align with their futures can seem daunting, especially in a world that bombards them with countless choices. But fear not, dads! With a bit of insight and some practical steps, you can confidently steer your children towards a fulfilling future.

First up, let's talk about the sheer variety of career options available today. Gone are the days when the choices seemed limited to becoming a doctor, lawyer, or engineer. Today, there are countless professions, from drone operators to digital marketers, cyber security specialists to sustainability experts. The world is continually evolving, creating new roles we couldn't even imagine a decade ago.

Start by exposing your children to this vast array of opportunities. Consider setting aside time each week to explore different careers together. This could be as simple as reading books, watching documentaries, or browsing career websites. The goal here is to broaden their horizons and spark curiosity about potential paths they might not have considered otherwise.

Next, let's dive into the importance of internships and volunteer opportunities. Internships provide invaluable hands-on experience and a taste of what working in a particular field might be like. They help bridge the gap between academic learning and real-world application, making them an excellent way for kids to test out their interests. Similarly, volunteering can offer experiences that shape career choices. Whether it's helping at a local animal shelter, participating in beach clean-ups, or assisting in community events, volunteering exposes kids to various fields and helps them build essential skills such as teamwork and leadership.

Encourage your children to pursue these opportunities but remember to keep the pressure low. Frame it as an adventure rather than a means to an end. This way, they can enjoy the process of discovery and learning without feeling burdened by expectations.

Educational pathways are another critical aspect to consider. With rising student debt and the financial pressures that come with it, making informed decisions regarding education and training is more important than ever. College isn't always the best route for everyone. Vocational schools, trade apprenticeships, and other forms of specialized training can offer rewarding careers without the hefty price tag.

Discuss these options openly with your children. Make sure they understand that pursuing alternative educational pathways isn't a sign of failure, but a strategic choice based on their unique interests and strengths. Share stories of successful individuals who took unconventional routes to success. By providing information and reassurance, you can help them make decisions that align with their aspirations and financial realities.

Supporting your children's aspirations and passions might be the most significant role you play in guiding their future. A father's support can make all the difference in whether a child's dream feels achievable. Show genuine interest in their hobbies and activities, and actively participate when possible. Whether it's attending recitals, going to art exhibits, or watching them code their first app, your involvement sends a powerful message of encouragement.

But remember, supporting their dreams doesn't mean dictating their path. It's tempting to project our own hopes and experiences onto our children, especially if our lives have taught us specific lessons. However, it's crucial to strike a balance between offering guidance and respecting their individuality. Ask open-ended questions to understand their thoughts and feelings better. Questions like "What excites you about this activity?" or "How does this align with what you want to do in the future?" can provide insights without being intrusive.

Fostering an environment where your children feel comfortable exploring their passions and making mistakes will build their confidence and resilience. Celebrate their successes, but also teach them how to learn from failures. This approach helps them develop a growth mindset, understanding that setbacks are part of the journey, not the end.

Finally, remember the power of leading by example. Demonstrate your passion and dedication through your actions. If you're enthusiastic about your work, continue learning, and seek new opportunities, your children are likely to adopt a similar attitude. Show them that pursuing one's interests can lead to a fulfilling and rewarding life.

In conclusion, guiding your children in identifying interests and paths that align with their futures involves exposing them to a variety of career options, encouraging hands-on experiences through internships and volunteering, discussing varied educational pathways, and wholeheartedly supporting their aspirations. By taking these steps, you'll empower your children to navigate their journey confidently and find their place in the world. So, roll up your sleeves, channel your inner mentor, and embark on this exciting adventure together. Your children's future starts with the insights and support you provide today!

Teaching Responsibility through Chores

Chores have long been a staple in households, providing more than just a clean home. They play a crucial role in teaching children accountability and the value of hard work. Assigning age-appropriate chores is an excellent starting point to build responsibility in children. For younger kids, simple tasks such as making their bed or putting toys away can set the groundwork. These small responsibilities gradually prepare them for more complex tasks as they grow. When children see that their actions contribute to the family's well-being, they begin to understand the importance of their role within the household.

Establishing routines is key to making chores an integral part of daily life. By incorporating chores into a consistent schedule, children learn to anticipate and complete tasks regularly. For example, creating a "when/then" routine, such as "When you hang up your coat after school, then you can have a snack," helps solidify these habits. The predictability of a routine can make the idea of chores less daunting and more manageable, allowing children to view them as a normal part of everyday life rather than a burdensome task.

Rewarding efforts and consistency in completing chores is vital in recognizing and motivating responsible behavior. Positive reinforcement can take many forms, from praise to tangible rewards like extra screen time or a special treat. This acknowledgment not only boosts self-esteem but also reinforces the connection between effort and reward. When children receive recognition for their hard work, they're more likely to continue exhibiting responsible behaviors, understanding that their contributions matter.

Mitigating resistance and instilling pride in doing chores are challenges many parents face. Children might initially resist chores due to a lack of interest or feeling overwhelmed by the tasks. One way to overcome this apathy is by switching jobs periodically. For instance, one child could clean a sibling's room while the other prepares a meal, adding an element of novelty and fun. Additionally, working together on chores can make them more enjoyable and foster a sense of teamwork. Phrases like "You put all your clothes in the basket! Great job!" go a long way in making children feel proud of their accomplishments.

The role of chores extends beyond mere household maintenance. Research suggests that engagement in chores can improve executive functions, including planning, self-regulation, task-switching, and memory. For younger children, self-care chores like making their bed are more manageable, while older children can handle both self-care and family-care tasks like helping with dishes. This gradual increase in responsibility helps children develop important cognitive skills and fosters a sense of independence.

Introducing chores should always be done positively, avoiding their use as punishment. Using chores as a form of discipline may yield short-term compliance but often results in resentment. Instead, presenting chores as an opportunity to contribute meaningfully to the family allows children to feel valued and significant. Reinforcing that their efforts help maintain the household creates a sense of purpose and belonging.

Keeping chores manageable is another essential aspect. Tasks that require only a short amount of time, about 10-15 minutes, are more likely to be repeated consistently compared to longer, more arduous chores. Making it a challenge or game can add excitement; for example, see how much can be cleaned in 15 minutes with some upbeat music in the background. Keeping the environment organized by reducing clutter can also make chores less overwhelming and more achievable for children.

Children thrive on challenges, so as they master certain tasks, it's beneficial to introduce more difficult chores to keep them engaged. If a child has learned to feed the family pet, add the responsibility of providing water or cleaning the pet's area. This method keeps them interested and continually developing new skills.

Ultimately, chores teach children essential life skills that extend beyond household duties. They learn to prioritize tasks, manage their time, and take ownership of their responsibilities. Whether it's setting the table, which builds self-esteem by showcasing their contribution, or engaging in household maintenance that improves executive function, chores are invaluable in personal development.

Creating an open dialogue about mistakes and learning from them is critical. As children navigate their chores, they will inevitably make errors. Encouraging open conversations about what went wrong and how to improve allows for constructive feedback and growth. This approach teaches resilience and the understanding that making mistakes is a part of the learning process.

Final Thoughts

To wrap things up, we've explored the importance of instilling core values and ethics in your children. By teaching them honesty, empathy, and respect, you give them the tools to navigate life's tricky mazes with confidence and integrity. Whether it's through bedtime stories or volunteer work, these lessons help shape their moral compass and build a strong foundation for adulthood. Remember, your actions speak louder than words—be the role model who walks the walk, so your kids can follow in those admirable footsteps.

But let's not stop there! Encouraging independence and problem-solving is just as crucial. From simple chores to tackling complex dilemmas, giving your kids responsibilities and the chance to flex their critical-thinking muscles sets them on a path to self-reliance. Praise their efforts, embrace their setbacks, and watch them grow into resilient problem-solvers. And hey, don't forget the power of a good chore list and a little bit of fun along the way. Who knew that something as simple as sorting laundry could teach so many life skills? So go ahead, mix in some humor, sprinkle a dash of patience, and support your kids as they learn and thrive.

CONCLUSION

As we come to the end of this journey, take a moment to reflect on all that you've faced and overcome. Remember the initial turbulence when everything changed—from hurried handovers at school gates to awkward moments at parent-teacher meetings. Those were no easy times. Through it all, you not only adapted but grew stronger, wiser, and more connected with your children. Each hurdle you've encountered has shaped both you and your relationship with your kids, highlighting the powerful bond you share.

Think back to those small victories that have punctuated your adventure—like the sheer joy on your child's face when they nailed that tricky science project. Or the pride you felt during that first Father's Day breakfast you started as a new tradition. These milestones are proof that even amid the chaos and adjustments, there are moments of pure joy worth celebrating. Every effort you've put into being a present and attentive father bears fruit in these precious experiences.

In maintaining strong relationships, it's essential to remember the importance of connection. Recall the simple yet profound moments when you sat down for dinner and discussed everything from school days to dreams for the future. It's in these casual conversations that deep connections are fostered. These moments provide your children with comfort and stability, showing them that despite other changes, your love and support remain constant.

And let's not forget about the co-parenting dance - a complicated tango requiring balance and patience. It may not always be easy, but working towards a cooperative relationship with your ex pays off in building a nurturing environment for your children. Consider those evenings spent side-by-side at your child's soccer game or school play. Such moments reinforce that, despite the separation, both parents can still create a united front for the sake of the kids.

Your journey doesn't stop here; parenting is an ongoing adventure that requires continuous learning and adapting. Just as you once navigated the tricky waters of introducing a new partner into your children's lives, you will constantly face situations that demand flexibility and growth. What works today might need tweaking tomorrow, and that's okay. It's all part of evolving as a parent and ensuring your approach remains fresh and effective.

In the realm of dating, remember that innovation and adaptation are your best friends. It's like juggling—sometimes you'll drop a ball, but each attempt makes you more skilled. Balancing your dating life and parenting duties isn't just possible; it's a chance to model for your children the art of healthy relationships and self-care. You are teaching them that it's important to find happiness and fulfillment while still honoring your responsibilities.

As we wrap up, let's talk about hope and resilience. Life as a divorced single father can indeed be challenging, but those challenges carve out pathways to deeper strengths and greater joys. Each setback is a setup for a comeback. And as you traverse these paths, you're equipping your children with invaluable lessons on overcoming adversity and chasing after resilience.

Picture yourself standing at the crossroads of this new chapter—you aren't merely surviving; you're thriving. Your journey is a testament to the power of hope, perseverance, and the relentless pursuit of a brighter future. Even when things seem overwhelming, remember how far you've come and all that you've achieved. The laughter, the tears, the sleepless nights pondering over decisions—you did it all and continue to do so because of love.

The road might twist and turn in unexpected ways, but that's the beauty of it. Embrace each new challenge with the same determination and humor that brought you this far. Keep celebrating the small wins, stay open to learning, and cherish every moment of connection. You're not alone—there's a whole tribe of fathers navigating similar terrains and rooting for your success.

In closing, know that this book isn't just a guide—it's a companion for your ongoing adventure. Whenever you need a reminder of your strength or a nudge toward optimism, flip through these pages. You've got this. Your kids see a superhero in you—their very own champion—and they're right. Every step you take now paves the way for a future filled with love, joy, and resilient hearts. So,

keep marching forward, dear father, with a smile, a dash of humor, and an unshakeable belief in yourself.

ABOUT THE AUTHOR

R.J. Aguilar, Jr. is a self-proclaimed and proud Disney Dad. For the better part of two decades, he has been a single dad, and an advocate for fathers all over the country who have struggled with the complexities and heartache of navigating divorce and co-parenting. Dr. Aguilar holds a Ph.D. in Theology, as well as a Juris Doctor. He specializes in divorce and custody mediation and is a Master Practitioner in Neuro-Linguistic Programming. He spends a good portion of his time speaking with estranged fathers in men's groups, churches, and prisons all over the United States.

 FriesenPress

One Printers Way
Altona, MB R0G 0B0
Canada

www.friesenpress.com

Copyright © 2025 by R.J. Aguilar, Jr.
First Edition — 2025

All rights reserved.

ISBN
978-1-03-914210-7 (Hardcover)
978-1-03-914209-1 (Paperback)
978-1-03-914211-4 (eBook)

1. FAMILY & RELATIONSHIPS, DIVORCE & SEPARATION

Distributed to the trade by The Ingram Book Company

www.ingramcontent.com/pod-product-compliance
Lightning Source LLC
LaVergne TN
LVHW091444040325
805029LV00001B/36